TRADE AMONG NATIONS

Dimensions • Proportions • Directions

TRADE AMONG NATIONS
Dimensions • Proportions • Directions

Michael Michaely
Hebrew University of Jerusalem, Israel

David Wajnryt
Central Bureau of Statistics, Israel

 **World Scientific**

NEW JERSEY · LONDON · SINGAPORE · BEIJING · SHANGHAI · HONG KONG · TAIPEI · CHENNAI · TOKYO

Published by

World Scientific Publishing Co. Pte. Ltd.

5 Toh Tuck Link, Singapore 596224

USA office: 27 Warren Street, Suite 401-402, Hackensack, NJ 07601

UK office: 57 Shelton Street, Covent Garden, London WC2H 9HE

Library of Congress Cataloging-in-Publication Data

Names: Michaely, Michael, author. | Wajnryt, David, author.

Title: Trade among nations : dimensions; proportions; directions / Michael Michaely, David Wajnryt.

Description: Hackensack : World Scientific, 2020. | Includes bibliographical references and index.

Identifiers: LCCN 2019049783 | ISBN 9789811213311 (hardcover)

Subjects: LCSH: International trade. | International economic integration.

Classification: LCC HF1379 .M523 2020 | DDC 382--dc23

LC record available at https://lccn.loc.gov/2019049783

British Library Cataloguing-in-Publication Data

A catalogue record for this book is available from the British Library.

For any available supplementary material, please visit
https://www.worldscientific.com/worldscibooks/10.1142/11639#t=suppl

Desk Editor: Ong Shi Min Nicole

Typeset by Stallion Press
Email: enquiries@stallionpress.com

Contents

List of Tables and Charts

Tables

Charts

Chapter 1

Introduction

General Framework

This book represents an empirical study of several salient attributes of the size and patterns of trade among nations. It primarily addresses the following: the <u>importance</u> of trade in a nation's economic activity, and its change over time; the <u>structural</u> attributes of trade flows; and the <u>directions</u> of these flows. These three general themes are explored in the seven chapters which form the core of the study, namely:

i. **Trade expansion**. This theme is analyzed in the study's first two chapters. <u>Chapter 2</u> addresses the growth of trade primarily through the measure of the foreign trade ratio, which is an indicator of the role of foreign trade in a country's aggregate economic activity. <u>Chapter 3</u> explores the impact on this process of expansion — positive or negative — of several crucial elements of the commodity and geographic structures of a country's trade, an issue to which the discussion under the following heading may also be partly related.

ii. **Structural attributes of global trade**. This theme is addressed in the following two chapters of the study. <u>Chapter 4</u> turns to an attribute to which some attention has been paid in the far past, but not in recent literature, the extent to which trade flows are concentrated in a small number of goods — or, to the contrary, are highly diversified. The feature addressed in <u>Chapter 5</u>, on the other hand, has attracted attention

1

often and repeatedly in studies of trade, namely, the importance of intra-industry trade as an element in global flows.

iii. **Directions of global trade**. This general theme is explored in the following three chapters. Chapter 6 addresses the impact of distance on the size of trade flows among nations. This issue is discussed in a multitude of studies in recent decades, but it is examined here in a different fashion, and yields largely different inferences from the conventional wisdom. Chapter 7 develops a scheme to estimate the level of distance traveled by trade flows of a country. Finally, Chapter 8 addresses the issue of the relative importance of trade within specific regions in the general scheme of global trade flows and inquires whether multilateral as opposed to bilateral trading bears a relationship to regional trading.

iv. Chapter 9 is of a different nature than the core of the study. In almost all of the elements the study has explored, **Europe** appears to have distinctly different attributes from the rest of the world. In this final chapter we assemble these unique attributes, often expanding on the discussions carried out in the thematic chapters. Furthermore, given the importance of Europe in world trade, we study elements of size, structure and direction specific to the trade of Europe.

Method

The study follows a uniform analytical approach. It presents not just the analysis of the attributes mentioned here, but also fundamental inter-relationships among them. It similarly explores the relationship of each phenomenon to basic attributes of an economy's nature: its level of economic development; its richness or poorness (expressed primarily in its level of per-capita income); its economic size (represented, similarly, by the country's aggregate product); its economic structure, primarily the extent of manufacturing in the economy's activity; and, finally, the country's location on the global map. In this final attribute, special attention is paid to the distinct role of Europe in determining trade patterns.

Most often, the study addresses both present position and developments over time, where "the present" is normally taken to be the year 2010, the latest year for which comprehensive data were available when the explorations of the study started (in one instance, for a component of the study which started early, this is replaced by 2008). The study covers, in principle, a period of fifty years — in a rough way, the latter half of the twentieth century. The starting year of the period is, thus, in principle, 1960. However, since many countries emerged as independent political entities only in the first half of the 1960's, the starting year of the period is often taken to be 1965 rather than 1960.

The study refers only to trade in <u>goods</u> and excludes trade in services. The latter has increased in importance in the last few decades; more services have become tradable, and new services have appeared that have been tradable since their inception. Similarly, the reporting of trade in services has improved. Yet, with regards to degree of classification, this reporting is not yet at the level to allow its empirical exploration in a manner similar to the analysis of trade in goods. Thus, for the purpose of this study, trade in services could not be included; hopefully, this should change in the near future.

We discuss here international "trade", but more often than not, we address only <u>exports</u>, rather than imports. Where needed, it is the analysis of exports vs. exports and imports combined, but not just imports as such. For many purposes, the rough equality of size of exports and imports would make the discussion of one where the other has already been addressed redundant. But, more importantly, the uniqueness of nations — the dissimilarity of one from another — is mostly much more predominant when the structure of exports rather than of imports is concerned. Hence our special attention to exports.

We conduct our analysis through the use of a variety of indices, coefficients and ratios: for convenience of expression we shall refer to all these measures of synthetic representation as "indices" — though, of course, some of them are not technically that. Some of these indices are taken from available literature; others, though they too would be found in the literature, had been presented in earlier studies of Michaely. But still others, probably the majority of instruments used here, have been developed and formulated first in the context of the present study. We regard this development as an important component of the contribution of the present study. To facilitate reference to the variety of indices, we have re-grouped them all (beyond their presentation in the context for which they serve) in a separate section. <u>Annex A</u> is a compendium of the indices, arranged by the order in which they are first presented in the study.

As stated, we very often discuss associations of attributes of trade with each other or with other characteristics of the economy. We normally do it by using a regression analysis, often a multiple regression. In these, we normally present the 'conventional' Pearson coefficient of correlation. But we always present also the outcome of a non-parametric analysis, expressed by Spearman rank correlation coefficients, which we commonly regard as the more meaningful representation of associations among the attributes at hand.

<u>Annex B</u> presents, for the benefit of potential future analysis or of critics, the statistical sources used for the exploration of the study.

Three of the book's chapters draw on articles previously published in the *Global Economy Journal.* Chapter 5 reproduces, with minor changes, the article on "Intra-Industry, Intra-Product, and Inter-Product Trade" (17/03/2017). Chapter 6 is an expanded version of "With Whom Do Nations Trade? — The Fading Distance" (2010, pp. 411–432). An embryonic version of Chapter 8 appeared as "Regionalism in Trade: An Overview of the Last Half Century" (2014, pp. 425–434).

Chapter 2

Trade Expansion: The Share of World Trade

Historical Background

The topic at hand scarcely suffers from neglect in the literature. Many observations and investigations have taken place in recent decades, and they almost universally indicate a rapid and consistent growth of the share of foreign trade in economic activity, in individual economies or in one or another aggregate of countries, for shorter or longer periods. However, apparently no <u>comprehensive</u> study observing the universe of world countries in sufficient detail and over an extended period is currently available. This will be the course of the present investigation, which will address practically all the world's countries and for the major part of the post-World War II (WWII) era.

To provide perspective, we start with a concise review of the available information regarding the subject matter at hand for a long period preceding the post war era, starting with the early post-industrial revolution and ending with the Second World War. The most comprehensive and thorough analysis of the trends of the foreign trade ratio (FTR) during this period is provided in the seminal study of Simon Kuznets (1967).[1] We

---

[1]The 'foreign trade ratio', a basic instrument of measurement in the present analysis, is the ratio of trade (exports, imports or, occasionally, their aggregate) to the nation's income (its GDP).

shall very briefly summarize here Kuznets' estimates. These are based on a variety of sources, involving a variety of methods and based on varying "baskets" of countries — inevitably (in view of availability of data) relatively more developed, more industrialized economies (i.e., economies which at the beginning of the period had already participated in the industrial revolution).

In synthesizing the available estimates, Kuznets came up with the following main inference: the foreign trade ratio (that is, the ratio of trade to product) increased remarkably over the observed period. Over the 19th century and early 20th century — from 1800 to 1913 — national product increased by 7.3 percent per decade, whereas foreign trade increased by 33 percent per decade. Hence, the ratio of trade to product increased by 24.3 percent per decade. This is obviously a very rapid change. To make it comparable with our forthcoming inferences for the half century following WWII, compound this rate as follows: it amounts to about a tripling of the foreign trade ratio over a period of 50 years, or to an increase by a factor of 9 over a century. The rise of the share was persistent over the period; it is found for every sub-period of a reasonable length (say, a decade) within the period. Although the rate of change was not uniform, it was always positive.

This trend was sharply reversed in the period from the eve of the First World War to the early years following the Second World War from 1913 to 1963 (the latest year for which data were available in the Kuznets' study), and the foreign trade ratio <u>fell</u> by about one third. Moreover, given that the trade ratio actually increased by about one quarter in the decade from 1953 to 1963, it appears that from the eve of World War I (WWI) to the early post-WWII years (early 1950's), the foreign trade ratio fell by almost a half. This was clearly the outcome of the two World Wars, the deep depression in between them, and the sharp change in trend of foreign trade policy from one largely following free trade to often a highly restrictive one during this period. It is partly in light of this fall that the resurgence of trade, which we shall witness later, should be viewed. But note, though, that even in the 'dark' 40 years from 1913 to 1953, the foreign trade ratio fell by roughly 16 percent per decade, substantially less (in absolute terms) than the aforementioned increase of close to 25 percent per decade in the preceding century.

Issues, Method and Coverage

The study will explore the performance of the foreign trade ratio over the last half century in the following way.

First — and of the most importance — the basic trend of change will be established for each individual country. Observations will be made for each single year and the trend over the period of 50 years will be inferred. The analysis will then turn from individual countries to the world's aggregates, to establish the global pattern of performances, and the potential role of specific countries in their impact on global patterns will be singled out.

Turning back to trends in individual countries, the relationship of the pattern of changes to several attributions of the <u>initial</u> position of countries will be analyzed. These attributes will be:

(i) The country's initial level of <u>per-capita</u> income. This is the best (though far from perfect) indicator of the economy's level of development. Similarly, it is a good proxy of the degree of the economy's industrialization.

(ii) The initial level of the country's <u>aggregate</u> income. This is a representation (arguably the best single one) of a country's economic <u>size</u>, an attribute which may be expected to play a role in determining the foreign trade ratio and its change.

(iii) The <u>initial level of the foreign trade ratio</u> itself. This part of the analysis will help to observe whether (high or low) relative levels of the ratio tend to be constant over time, to increase, or, to the contrary, be reversed.

A separate section of the study will then address the impact of changes of (relative) <u>prices</u> on the apparent trends revealed in the earlier analysis. That is, estimates at <u>constant</u> vs. <u>current</u> prices will be contrasted.

In principle, the study should cover <u>all of</u> the world's countries. Several constraints, however, slightly narrow this universe. To make estimates for the period 1960–2010, data for these years are obviously required. To be as inclusive as reasonably possible, we sometimes cut corners. We occasionally replaced the year 1960 as the starting point with some other early 1960s year, when data availability led to this (mainly when political entities became independent only in the early 1960s). We also made some arbitrary decisions about the identity of countries (e.g., regarding post-unification Germany as a continuation of the pre-1990 Federal Republic). The most important exclusions are countries which, until 1990, had formed the Soviet Union and its Warsaw Pact partners, as well as the components of the former Yugoslavia. Altogether, the study covers 95 countries. In their aggregate, they contributed close to 90 percent of world income and 83 percent of world trade in 2010 (in 1960 the ratios were similar; they contributed close to 83 percent for both world income and world trade).[2]

Findings

We start by estimating the foreign trade ratios (FTRs) for each individual country for each single year from 1960 to 2010. Presenting these estimates here, either through tables or through charts, would take up too much space. We find it sufficient to present, in Annex Table A.1, the data for each 10th year, starting in 1960. We note that these data provide evidence of a clear and distinct trend of <u>rising</u> FTRs over the period. This trend is shared by the large majority of countries: only in 9 countries is the trend negative, and even there it is weak. In most countries the (positive) trend is persistent. The year-to-year changes (not shown) do point out fluctuations, but those may often be due to price movements rather than to changes in real activity, fluctuations of oil prices being the most obvious element. The stages of the business cycle are another common cause for fluctuations; sharp declines of the FTR in the latest years of the period surveyed provide an illustration of such a relationship and reflect the global economic crisis of these years.

Next, we move from the performance of individual countries to developments in the universe of countries as a whole, or large segments of it.

---

[2] Unless specified otherwise we use here, for the sake of convenience, the term "world" to refer to the universe of (95) countries studied here, although the trade of this "universe" provided in 2010 does not capture the whole of world trade but its only overwhelming parts.

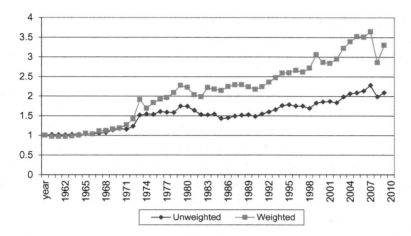

Chart 2.1:   Mean change of FTR, unweighted and weighed

For this purpose, the individual annual estimates of the FTRs are aggregated into global indices; that is, an FTR for the universe of 95 countries is constructed on an annual basis. The outcome is presented by means of Chart 2.1. Here, two aggregate indices are shown. One is the arithmetic average, where each country estimate is counted equally. The other is a <u>weighted</u> average of the individual ratios, with weights assigned by the share of each country in world (i.e., the aggregate of 95 countries) <u>income</u>, in the start year (1960). The initial level of the ratio (i.e., in 1960) is represented as unity.

The global trend is, once more, clear cut. Looking, first, at the unweighted average, it appears that it <u>doubled</u> over the period under review (the mean change of the countries' FTR was precisely 2). Once more, the change seems to be persistent, though with fluctuations which must, again, reflect to a large extent changes in oil prices (such as their sharp rise from 1973 to 1980 and decline over the following decade). The <u>weighted</u> average — presenting the change of the share of trade in the world as a whole — provides an even much more glaring evidence of an increase: the level of this share more than <u>tripled</u> over the half century under review.

Curiously, this appears to be almost identical with the rate of increase of the FTR per half century indicated earlier in the Kuznets estimates for the 19th Century. Thus, if one ignores the "dark period" between the break of WWI and the end of WWII, a rate of increase of the FTR by a factor of 3 per half century would appear to represent the whole long period of two centuries from the early days of the industrial revolution to the end of the 20th century.

The (positive) difference between the weighted and unweighted means indicates, of course, that some countries which weigh heavily (in their world income shares) witnessed particularly large increases in their FTRs. Indeed, much of this reflects the impact of a single country — the USA. This country, the world's largest (in terms of aggregate income) even today, represented in the base year (1960) as much as 43 percent of the world's aggregate income (in 2010 it was around 23 percent). And the expansion of its trade was particularly strong.

The role of the USA as of other parts of the world is highlighted by means of Chart 2.2. This shows four graphs representing changes in the FTRs over the period for three 'blocs' as well as for the 'world' as a whole. One 'bloc' is the USA, another is Europe,[3] and the third the rest of the world. The FTRs of the latter two 'blocs' constitute, for each, the <u>weighted</u> average of the bloc's members. The exceptional performance of the USA is again vividly shown in this graph. On the other hand, perhaps

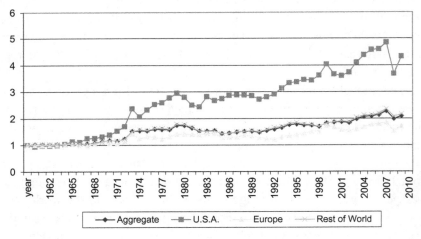

Chart 2.2: Change of FTR by major blocs

---

[3] "Europe" includes: Austria, Belgium, Denmark, Finland, France, Germany, Iceland, Italy, Netherlands, Norway, Portugal, Spain, Sweden, Switzerland, and the UK.

contrary to what intuition would indicate, "Europe" stands out as being the group with the <u>smallest</u> expansion of its foreign trade ratio. While Europe has, throughout the period, been the world's largest trading bloc and remains so, the share of foreign trade in its economic activity, though increasing by itself, manifests a <u>decline</u> in comparison with the performance of trade in other countries (most glaringly, in comparison with the trade performance in the USA). This observation checks with what we shall indicate later about the convergence of foreign trade ratios.

We now turn to a summary measure on which our further analysis will be based, namely, the change of the FTR from the beginning of the period to its end. Table 2.1 presents this change for each of the 95 countries analyzed here. To avoid the risk of excessive dependence on data for single years, where annual fluctuations may always introduce distortions, we compare not 2010 with 1960 but five-year averages — namely, the change from 1960–1964 to 2006–2010. In practical terms, this may still be referred to as the change 'over the last half century'. To get an impression at a glance, countries are arranged in Table 2.1 not by alphabetical order but by the descending order of the ratio by which their FTRs increased over the period. Two inferences from these data are clearly suggested.

First, a remarkable increase of the FTR took place over the period, and it was almost universal. Of the 95 countries, the FTR increased in 80 or 81. In eight of the countries it may be judged to have remained roughly stable; only in six or seven countries did the rate clearly fall. The unweighted ratio about doubled, on average for the 95 countries (the mean ratio of increase was 1.94, and the median 1.79). This clearly agrees with the inference drawn earlier.

Second, though the relative size of trade appears to have expanded almost universally, a large degree of <u>variance</u> in the performance of individual countries still exists. At one extreme, the country's FTR increased by factors of 5 to 8. At the lower end of the distribution, on the other hand, the FTR <u>fell</u> over the period by about one third. Yet, the distribution is quite heavily concentrated; for close to two thirds of the countries, the FTR increased by a ratio roughly within the range of 1.5 to 3, indicating a significant increase of the relative size of trade.

We move to examine the relationship between the rate of change of a country's FTR, over the period as a whole, and several country attributes

Table 2.1:   Change in foreign trade ratio
(Ratio of average 2006–2010 to average 1960–1964)

China	7.57	Rwanda	2.31	Greece	1.72	Peru	1.23
Seychelles	5.25	Togo	2.27	Nepal	1.71	Brazil	1.19
Turkey	4.59	Lesotho	2.19	Nigeria	1.65	Sierra Leone	1.19
USA	4.53	Zimbabwe	2.19	Jamaica	1.62	Singapore	1.19
Cambodia	4.36	Madagascar	2.15	Afghanis.	1.61	Oman	1.17
Bahrain	4.03	Morocco	2.14	Finland	1.61	Sri Lanka	1.17
Mexico	3.61	El Salvador	2.10	Papua N. G.	1.53	Venezuela	1.16
Mauritania	3.60	Panama	2.09	Israel	1.49	Zambia	1.15
Thailand	3.49	Senegal	2.09	S. Africa	1.49	Pakistan	1.14
Argentina	3.12	Chile	2.08	Liberia	1.45	Kuwait	1.12
Burundi	3.09	Austria	2.06	Switzer.	1.43	Denmark	1.09
Chad	3.08	Tunisia	2.04	Australia	1.42	Iceland	1.02
Korea Rep.	3.02	Bolivia	2.02	Cameroon	1.42	Belize	0.94
Honduras	2.99	Germany	1.96	Egypt A. R.	1.42	Sudan	0.94
Burkina Faso	2.96	Costa Rica	1.95	Fiji	1.42	Bahrain	0.92
Guatemala	2.89	Malaysia	1.94	Kenya	1.42	St. Vincent	0.88
Ecuador	2.76	Portugal	1.94	Netherlands	1.41	Barbados	0.87
Benin	2.66	Italy	1.92	UK	1.40	Gabon	0.81
India	2.64	Uruguay	1.86	Colombia	1.35	Cen. Afr. Rep.	0.74
Hong Kong	2.62	Domin. Rep.	1.83	Japan	1.35	Algeria	0.73
Belgium	2.61	Malawi	1.83	Cote d'Ivoire	1.34	St. Kitts. Ne.	0.71
Philippines	2.49	Canada	1.80	Ghana	1.30	Congo Rep.	0.65
Iraq	2.39	Nicaragua	1.79	Uganda	1.29	Trin. & Tobago	0.60
France	2.37	Sweden	1.76	Swaziland	1.26		

which may be relevant. These are, partly at least, suggested by a-priori elements surveyed in an earlier section. Three such relationships are examined: in all of them, the 'attributes' are represented by quantitative indications which refer to the starting point of the period (i.e., 1960). In this analysis the background should always be remembered — we are dealing with a period in which the world as a whole, and the clear majority of its individual countries, exhibited a particularly high rate of economic growth.

Three potential relationships are examined.

(i)   Is the intensity of expansion of the FTR related to the country's <u>size</u> (best indicated by aggregate GDP)? Small countries, as we well know, tend to have higher FTRs. As Kuznets indicated, while this holds for <u>cross-section</u> comparisons, it does <u>not</u> follow that as countries grow, their FTRs tend to fall. Here we examine a slightly different angle: Do large (or small) countries, at the entry point, tend to expand their trade more than others?

(ii) Do <u>rich</u> (or poor) countries (as indicated by levels of per-capita GDP) tend to have a particularly strong (or weak) expansion of their trade? We shall note later, in interpreting the study's findings, that on this score the <u>a-priori</u> prediction is not clear-cut.

(iii) Finally, how is the rate of expansion of trade related to the <u>initial</u> level of the FTR? That is, do countries which exhibit a high trade ratio to start with tend to demonstrate a further rise of the relative position of the FTR with time, or is it the other way around? The issue partly overlaps, presumably, with the one examined under (i): If larger countries tend to have initially lower FTRs, the distinction between the issues of initial economic <u>size</u> and that of initial levels of the FTR tends to become partly blurred.[4]

The relationships at hand are analyzed through the use of the Spearman rank correlation coefficient, which represents the degree of proximity of the <u>ranking</u> of each country in each of the three respective orders (of the initial levels of aggregate income, per-capita income, and the foreign trade ratio) with the country's ranking in the order of the level of increase of its FTR over the half-century concerned. These coefficients are presented in Table 2.2.

Given the large number of observations, all coefficients are significant at practically any desired level. But they obviously represent a different

---

[4] Another relationship which might have been examined is that between the <u>ratio of economic growth</u>, over the period, and the rate of expansion of the FTR. However, while for the other (three) relationship causality could only be in one direction, here it may be two-way: rapid economic growth could encourage rapid growth of trade, but it could also work the other way around (the impact of trade expansion on growth has been extensively discussed in the literature). We therefore avoid here the examination of this specific relationship.

Table 2.2: Spearman rank correlation coefficient, three series with the change of FTR.

Series of (1)	Correlation with the Increase of FTR (2)
1. Initial level of aggregate income	0.201
2. Initial level of per-capita income	−0.109
3. Initial level of FTR	−0.421

intensity of compatibility of the series. The first coefficient is <u>positive</u>, indicating that the larger the country in terms of aggregate income, the <u>more</u> the level of its FTR should tend to rise. But the relationship is weak and, as noted before, may be associated with what soon will be noted about the coefficient of the third series. The second coefficient indicates that the higher the initial level of a country's per-capita income — the richer and, presumably, the more industrialized it is — the <u>lower</u> the relative expansion of its foreign trade. But this relationship appears to be particularly weak. It does not lend support to any of the <u>a-priori</u> claims — which, we shall note later, pointed out in conflicting directions. Finally, the third coefficient is <u>negative</u> and provides a clear, rather than weak, indication. It represents a tendency for the FTRs to <u>converge</u>; the lower the initial level of the ratio, the <u>stronger</u> its tendency to increase over the period. This observation seems to be important, though we cannot suggest an <u>a-priori</u> explanation for it.[5]

Removing the Price Effect: Constant-Prices Estimates[6]

Up to now, all values of economic activity (income, trade) have been recorded at <u>current</u> prices, mixing changes in "real" quantities and changes in prices.[7]

---

[5] The well-known "regression fallacy" always looms in the background, but we see no reason why this should be suspected here.
[6] To avoid confusion, we deal here with the <u>accounting</u> aspect of price changes, <u>not</u> the impact of price changes on economic activities.
[7] "Prices" refer to, in the present context, <u>relative prices</u>: equi-proportional price change in all activities would be immaterial where, as in here, <u>shares</u> are concerned.

Abstracting from price changes would obviously be desirable in short-term comparisons, where price fluctuations may be strong (particularly in trade in resource-based goods, energy products being an extreme and important case) and may easily distort inferences about the "real" activity of the economy. But even beyond it, addressing long-term comparisons as we do here, the impact of price changes may be expected to be important, and separating the estimates of "real" performance from it should be desirable.

It is generally assumed that with economic growth, the relative price of tradable to non-tradable activities should tend to <u>fall</u>.[8] This is based on <u>a-priori</u> analysis and is supported by several empirical observations.[9] This presumption has a long tradition. Among its manifestations, the so-called "Scandinavian Model" of inflation is based on it. Perhaps the most notable development it has led to — though in <u>cross-section</u> rather than in over-time comparisons — is the construction of the "purchasing power parity" rate of exchange, arguably the most important innovation in national accounting in recent decades.

With the most remarkable economic progress over the half century reviewed here, a significant fall of the relative price of tradable to non-tradable activities should thus be expected. Prices of "trade" might reasonably be expected to move simultaneously with prices of "tradables"; whereas the price of "income" is some combination of prices of tradable and non-tradable activities. Hence, a fall of the relative price of tradables should find an expression in a fall of the relative price of trade to income and, in our estimates, to a fall of the foreign trade ratio, i.e. the proportion of trade to income. Abstraction from this impact should thus lead to estimates showing a <u>larger</u> increase (or a smaller fall) of the FTRs over the period under review.

<u>A-priori</u> analysis indicates that neither the current-prices nor the constant-prices estimates would yield the "true" measure of the change one would want to estimate; the latter falls somewhere in between the two, at a place which <u>cannot</u> be pointed out by analysis.[10] The constant-prices

---

[8] In addition, if relative transportation costs in <u>international</u> trade did indeed fall, this should lower the estimated share of trade at current prices.

[9] See, for instance, Michaely. (1981, 1984)

[10] The <u>a-priori</u> analysis, as well as empirical illustrations, may be found in Michaely, <u>ibid</u>.

estimates, to which we now turn, thus do not provide, by themselves, a "true" indicator of the change we want to measure.[11] But their observation would provide one boundary, the other being that yielded by the current prices estimates.[12]

Estimates of the change in the relative price of tradables to non-tradables are not readily available, nor are the raw data on which such estimates may be based, for the large collection of countries which is addressed here. Instead, we use two proxies which, at least in their combination, may serve adequately for the purpose.

(i) **Method A:** This method is based on the use of the system of national accounts. By this procedure, we divide the change in the foreign trade ratio yielded by current-prices estimates by that yielded by constant-prices estimates. This provides the size of the relative-price change of "trade" (in our case, imports) to that of the national product — the index we are looking for. This procedure might have been ideal for the purpose, except for two qualifications. One is that in moving from current-prices to constant-prices estimates, the makers of the accounting systems in the individual countries must have used a variety of schemes, probably of limited reliability on many occasions. But this qualification is of no pragmatic inference. In a study like the present, the use of data constructed by the individual countries is unavoidable. The other qualification: the national-accounting systems refer to the shares of the trade in goods and services, whereas the present study refers only to trade in goods. But we may venture a guess that this difference is generally only of little significance. Trade in goods alone generally constituted — at least over the period concerned — a much larger volume than trade in services. Moreover, price changes of "services" are mostly difficult to construct and are

---

[11] This analysis also indicates that if, for one reason or another, we had to choose only one of the two methods of estimation, the constant-prices estimate would be preferable.

[12] Simon Kuznets' estimates (in 1964) — based, as they were, on a variety of sources for a variety of periods — involved both current-prices and constant-prices data (the latter derived, essentially, from estimates of changes in volumes of activities). Among later contributions, the need for constant-prices estimates (and some sample empirical indication) is mentioned in Rosecrance and Stein (1973).

sometimes even difficult to define. It is a reasonable hunch to expect that on many occasions, the estimates concerned simply applied the price change of trade in goods alone to the more inclusive trade in goods and services. This method provides data for 48 countries.

(ii) **Method B:** This is an attempt to estimate the relative price change not strictly of "trade" but of "tradables".[13] It is yielded by the relative change of the <u>consumer price</u> index by that of the <u>wholesale price</u> (the latter often being designated by other, close-by terms). Prices of tradable goods may be assumed to be quite closely approximated by wholesale prices. Consumer prices, on the other hand, also cover prices of strictly <u>domestic</u> activities, be it those directly serving the consumers or those added to the tradable activities (such as, for instance, domestic retailing or transportation services). Thus, wholesale prices may be presumed to be a good proxy of the price of tradables, whereas consumer prices may stand for the price of national product (or national income).[14] Use of this method provides 28 observations.

These two methods combined thus provide 76 observations. Of these, 28 countries are common to both lists. Thus, in combination, estimates for 58 countries are provided by these two methods of estimation.[15] Whether it is legitimate to combine findings of the two alternative estimates is an issue that will be dealt with shortly, after the findings are reviewed and analyzed. The estimates yielded by the two methods are presented in Table 2.3.

The two alternative estimates designated by Method A and Method B — the "national accounts" method (NAC) and the "consumer-wholesale prices" method (c/w.p.) are presented in, respectively, columns (1) and (2). Several inferences emerge.

---

[13] Consult Michaely (1981).

[14] For a more thorough analysis of this issue, Michaely (1981, 1984) may be consulted.

[15] Of these, six countries are not covered in the main analysis of the study: Bangladesh, Congo Dem. Rep., Guatemala, Iran Isl. Rep., Luxembourg, and New Zealand. They are recorded in the table both for the sake of illustrating price movements <u>per se</u>, and for the potential benefit of further studies.

Table 2.3: Relative prices and constant-prices estimates
(2010 relative to 1960)

	Index of Relative Price of Non-tradables			Change of FTR	
	Method A (NAC) (1)	Method B (c/w.p) (2)	Combined (3)	At Current Prices (4)	At Constant Price = (4) × (3) (5)
* Australia	1.91	1.34	1.91	1.42	2.72
* Austria	1.57	0.74	1.57	2.06	3.23
Bangladesh	0.34	—	0.34	—	—
* Belgium	1.28	—	1.28	2.61	3.33
Benin	0.88	—	0.88	2.67	2.34
Brazil	0.94	0.52	0.94	1.19	1.12
* Canada	1.34	1.24	1.34	1.80	2.42
Chile	1.21	—	1.21	2.09	2.54
Colombia	1.52	1.17	1.52	1.35	2.06
Congo Dem. Rep.	0.88	—	0.88	—	—
Congo Rep.	1.68	—	1.68	0.65	1.09
Costa Rica	1.31	0.72	1.31	1.95	2.55
* Denmark	2.78	1.67	2.78	1.09	3.01
Dominican Rep.	0.61	—	0.61	1.83	1.12
Ecuador	1.25	—	1.25	2.75	3.45
Egypt Arab Rep.	0.49	1.41	0.49	1.42	0.70
* Finland	1.47	1.37	1.47	1.61	2.37
* France	1.88	—	1.88	2.37	4.44
Gabon	1.69	—	1.69	0.81	1.37
* Greece	2.10	—	2.10	1.72	3.61
Guatemala	0.39	—	0.39	—	—
Honduras	0.44	—	0.44	2.09	1.32
* Iceland	1.94	—	1.94	1.02	1.98

(*Continued*)

Table 2.3:   *(Continued)*

	Index of Relative Price of Non-tradables			Change of FTR	
	Method A (NAC) (1)	Method B (c/w.p) (2)	Combined (3)	At Current Prices (4)	At Constant Price = (4) × (3) (5)
India	0.92	1.20	0.92	2.65	2.44
Iran Isl. Rep.	—	1.06	1.06	—	—
* Ireland	—	1.92	1.92	0.90	1.73
* Italy	1.72	—	1.72	1.92	3.31
* Japan	2.76	2.64	2.76	1.42	3.92
Kenya	0.69	—	0.69	1.48	0.99
* Korea Rep.	3.67	1.58	3.67	3.02	11.07
Lesotho	0.67	—	0.67	2.19	8.43
* Luxembourg	1.08	—	1.08	—	—
Malaysia	0.89	—	0.89	1.94	1.72
Mauritania	0.71	—	0.71	1.92	1.35
Mexico	1.59	1.58	1.59	3.61	5.74
Morocco	0.97	—	0.97	2.14	2.07
* Netherlands	2.44	1.58	2.44	1.41	3.44
* New Zealand	—	1.06	1.06	—	—
Nicaragua	1.90	—	1.90	1.89	3.02
* Norway	1.88	0.98	1.88	0.69	1.30
Pakistan	—	0.73	0.73	1.14	0.83
Panama	—	0.77	0.77	2.09	1.61
Peru	1.46	—	1.46	1.23	1.79
Philippines	0.57	—	0.57	2.49	1.41
* Portugal	1.67	—	1.67	1.93	3.22
Rwanda	2.41	—	2.42	2.32	5.61
Senegal	0.41	—	0.41	2.09	0.86

(Continued)

Table 2.3:   *(Continued)*

	Index of Relative Price of Non-tradables			Change of FTR	
	Method A (NAC) (1)	Method B (c/w.p) (2)	Combined (3)	At Current Prices (4)	At Constant Price = (4) × (3) (5)
South Africa	1.17	0.96	1.17	1.49	1.75
* Spain	2.90	2.23	2.90	2.79	8.08
* Sweden	1.30	—	1.30	1.76	2.28
* Switzerland	—	1.92	1.92	1.43	2.74
Syrian Arab Rep.	—	1.21	1.21	—	—
Thailand	—	0.86	0.86	3.41	2.93
Togo	0.51	—	0.51	2.23	1.13
Tunisia	—	0.78	0.78	—	—
* USA	—	1.26	1.26	4.53	5.73
Uruguay	1.43	1.15	1.43	1.86	2.66
Zambia	1.64	—	1.64	1.16	1.90

As we shall note soon, the average and median levels of the price increases are somewhat higher when Method A is considered. But the order of price movements is quite similar; the Spearman rank correlation between the two series is 0.664 (excluding the extreme case of Egypt, it would rise to 0.750). This level of concordance should tend to strengthen the reliability of the use of either method. It also indicates that combining the two methods — creating a series in which one method complements the other — should be a legitimate procedure. This is done in column (3) of the table. Here, when only a single country estimate is available by one method or the other, this is taken to be "the" index of price movement; whereas when estimates are recorded by both methods, the estimate yielded by Method A (the NAC) is adopted, and recorded in column (3), as the proper representation in the "combined" series. By "Method A" 48 countries are recorded and by "Method B" 28 countries. Of these, we noted that 18 countries appear in both lists. Thus, the combined list recorded in column (3) includes 58 countries.[16]

The price trend revealed by the estimates in Table 2.3 is unmistakable regardless of whether Method A, Method B, or the combined data are considered. Method A yields an average price index of 1.40, and a median of 1.31; by Method B, the average is 1.23 and the median is 1.20; in the combined series, the average is 1.36 and the median is 1.28. The variation of the price data is quite large. In some cases, the (relative) price increase is extremely high; for example, it reaches a level of 3.67 in the Korea Republic. What <u>is</u> uniform, though, is that the price movement at hand is in one direction — an increase. Rarely do we see a <u>fall</u> of the index, and even indices around unity are not common. The <u>a-priori</u> expectation that the relative price of non-tradables should rise with time (or its obverse, that the price of tradables should fall) is thus fully borne out.

It follows directly from this finding that the increase of the FTR over the period should be substantially higher when estimates are made at constant rather than current prices. In Table 2.3, column (4) copies from Table 2.1 the estimates of the changes in FTR which, of course, have been made using <u>current</u> prices data. Multiplying each such estimate by the estimated relative price change (column (3)) yields the change in the FTR at <u>constant</u> prices.[17] These estimates are recorded in column (5).

Given that the relative price of income to trade increased substantially (i.e., the relative price of trade declined), it follows that the estimated

---

[16] In the procedure followed in Method B price estimates, weights used in moving from "current" to "constant" prices were shifting, though not necessarily from year to year. Presumably, this must also be mostly true for the individual country estimates on which Method A is based. Thus, the move from current to constant prices <u>is not</u> based on the use of the starting year (1960 or around it) for weights (nor on the use of the final year prices).

[17] Designate: Δ FTR (curr.) = change in FTR at current price.

Δ FTR (con.) = change in FTR at constant price.

$\Delta \frac{P(n)}{P(t)}$ = change in relative price of income to trade.

Hence:

$$\Delta \text{ FTR (curr.)} = \Delta \text{ FTR (con.)} \times \Delta \frac{P(t)}{P(n)}$$

$$\therefore \Delta \text{ FTR (cons.)} = \Delta \text{ FTR (cur.)} \times \Delta \frac{P(n)}{P(t)}$$

changes in the FTR show a much more impressive increase, over the period, when made at constant rather than current prices. For the 50 countries for which data are recorded in column (5) the average and median index of change of the FTR are, respectively, 1.91 and 1.92 when estimated at current prices; when estimates are made at constant prices, the average and median values are 2.83 and 2.39. In other words, the shift from estimating the movements at current prices to the use of constant prices raises the estimated increase of the FTR by almost 50 percent over this 50-year period. This is a radical change in our view of how the role of trade, or the extent of globalization, has changed over the period.

Of perhaps no lesser interest should be the distinction among countries by income level. Of the 58 countries for which relative-price estimates are recorded in column (3), 22 will be classified as "high-income", with asterisks attached to their names. The mean ratio of price change for this group is 1.90; and the median is 1.88; for the "rest", the remaining 36 countries, the mean and median are, in turn, 1.03 and 0.92. Thus, the phenomenon of (impressive) increase of the relative price of income to trade is confined, so far as groups are concerned, to high-income countries, in which the relative price at hand almost <u>doubled</u> over the period. For the rest, this price remained practically unchanged. This agrees with the <u>a-priori</u> expectation that the relative price concerned should increase with the levels of income and development. This contrast in the record of movement of relative prices is directly reflected in the gap between estimates of the change of FTR at constant vis-à-vis current prices. In column (4) and (5), these estimations by the two alternative methods are recorded for 50 countries, of which 22 are "high-income" and 28 are the "rest" — that is, middle- and low-income countries. For the high-income countries, the estimated average and median changes are 1.88 and 1.76 at current prices, and they increase to as much as 3.70 and 3.23 when estimated at constant prices. For the other group, the estimated values are, respectively, 1.85 and 1.92 when made at current prices, and they change only a little, to 2.26 and 1.79, when estimated at constant prices.

These findings illuminate an important issue raised earlier in the study, namely, when countries that are already highly developed advance further, should their degree of openness to the world — their FTR — be expected to rise or to fall? We shall address this issue, among others, in the following, concluding section. Our findings clearly indicate that "Sombart's Law" was wrong.

Expectations and Inferences

Having established in our analysis the extent and nature of the change of the foreign trade ratio over the last half century, we turn to a survey of what may have been the sources of this change. To start with, we shall pose an a-priori question — an ex-ante one: At any given period, what would be the potential factors expected to affect the foreign trade ratio one way or another?

Such factors, or forces, belong in essence to two categories. One is the basket of elements which lead to economic performance that should have an impact on foreign trade and the foreign trade ratio. The other is the basket of policy measures, assembled under the term "trade policy", which should affect this performance. We start with discussing the latter, trade policies which conceptually should have a clear, straightforward impact. In essence, the nature of this impact is obvious: the freer is the foreign trade of barriers, the larger is this trade and the higher the foreign trade ratio. Difficulties would arise when estimation of the level of trade barriers is attempted, a subject matter with which the present analysis does not deal. Quantifying the level of a barrier would normally be complicated, even in the presumably simple case of estimating the level of barriers through tariffs. One may potentially resort to a practice of observing changes in the level of barriers merely on an ordinal, rather than cardinal scale — that is, not establishing a numerical level of barriers, but only asking whether the level of barriers went up or down. This would be possible when all policy measures moved in the same direction, or at least when some changed in one direction and none in the opposite. Otherwise, a quantification of individual policies would still be required.

During the period analyzed, however, such measurement issues are not of much importance; the developments leave no doubt. The global performance on this score is so clear-cut that, so far as general trends are concerned, it does not require much of an empirical verification. By the middle of the 20th century the world was probably more riddled by barriers and constraints on — and government intervention in — foreign trade than at any other time during the preceding century, including even the inter-war period; that is, at any time since the emergence of the industrial world. Free (or nearly free) foreign trade was practically nonexistent. Trade was heavily restricted by tariffs, non-tariff barriers, foreign-exchange controls, state trading, barter or clearing agreements, and various similar devices. Relaxation of all these barriers has been dramatic, though gradual rather than instantaneous. By the end of the 20th century, world trade must have been mostly characterized as "free" rather than "managed", with restrictions still applied, in the industrial world, mainly in the agricultural sector. Foreign trade may not yet be as free as towards the end of the 19th century (this <u>does</u> require an empirical evidence). A major force working for free trade at that earlier time was the policy of the UK, the world's economic (and trade) leader through-out the century. Such leadership is missing today; the USA, the largest economy, is neither as predominant in world trade nor as devoted to the free-trade policy as the UK was earlier. Such considerations may be relevant for comparisons of recent performance with those of the 19th century, but there is no doubt as to how the change in trade policies should have affected foreign trade over the last half century. This must be crucial for predicting an increased role of foreign trade over the period reviewed here.

We move now to a discussion of the inherent factors which may lead to economic performance biased towards to or away from increasing the share of trade in aggregate economic activity. We may perhaps best start with mentioning what might be termed the "organizing principle" of such performance, as it was expounded in the fundamental analysis of Simon Kuznets. This was stated as follows:

"The long-term changes in the foreign-trade proportion in the course of economic growth may be viewed as the outcome of competition between the factors which induce growth of domestic activity and those that induce growth of foreign trade. ... [Hence] we must identify the factors that were effective in inducing foreign trade than of domestic output." [Kuznets, <u>op cit, p. 24</u>]

Note the emphasis on the <u>competition</u>: for the foreign trade ratio to increase it is not enough to identify factors which contribute to the growth of trade (such as increased productivity in the process of producing and moving traded goods); but that such changes should <u>not</u> be matched by equal or even larger changes in factors which encourage <u>other</u> activities.

First, in a most obvious way, comes to mind the change of <u>transportation costs</u>. These, in all probability, have gone down. This is definitely true for transportation by air, which barely existed at the middle of the 20th century; however, it also holds, in all likelihood, for transportation by land and by sea. But this trend by itself, assuming it has indeed existed, does not predict the performance of <u>foreign</u> trade. For such a prediction two other elements would be required. First, for the activity of trade in general, we recall, from Kuznets, that to increase the proportion of trade transportation costs would have to decline more than (or relative to) costs involved in other activities, and on this, no <u>a-priori</u> presumption would offer itself. Second, supposing such a <u>relative</u> decline of transportation costs has indeed taken place, how would such a change affect the proportion of <u>foreign</u> trade in the trade activity as a whole?

An obvious element that would be required to answer this question is whether the decline of transportation costs is biased, by its nature, for or against international trade vs. domestic trade. No guess on this issue may be ventured here (though a feasible research of this subject might provide some indication). Suppose, with no prior knowledge, that <u>no</u> such relative change has taken place, e.g., to take the simplest case, that transportation costs have gone down equally in all production activities. Would such a presumption still offer any inference about the relative impact on <u>foreign</u> trade? Here, a classification of countries by nature of size and distance may be of some use.

a. The home country is <u>large</u>, in terms of territory, and its major trading partners are <u>close</u> by (e.g., Canada). In this case the reduction of transportation costs is more important for the country's domestic trade; hence, it is biased <u>against</u> foreign trade.
b. The country is <u>large</u> and its trading partners are <u>distant</u> (e.g., China). In this case, the change in costs is "neutral" (in the sense that no <u>a-priori</u> expectation is yielded).
c. The country is <u>small</u>, and its trading partners are <u>distant</u> (Singapore would probably be the perfect example here). The change in costs, in this case, is obviously biased <u>towards</u> foreign trade.
d. Finally, the economy is <u>small</u> (in terms of territory) and its trade partners are <u>nearby</u> (the Netherlands would be a good example here).

In this category, the change in transportation costs would be "neutral" (in the sense mentioned before).

All these a-priori observations may be useful in analyzing individual countries. However, without much detailed information (and without, presumably, much further research), they would not lead to an obvious a-priori prediction of the impact of changes in transportation costs on the global change of the share of trade over the half century under consideration. Thus, while changes in transportation costs would presumably be of much importance in determining changes in the role of foreign trade, we suggest no guess on this score.

Another element of determination of the global share of trade, on Kuznets' list, is the opening of new territories. During the last half century, similarly to the 19th century, such process must have indeed taken place, though, presumably, on a smaller scale. Parts of South and Southeast Asia may belong in this category. However, a methodological issue arises; should we count this as a separate element or just as one of the manifestations of the change, discussed earlier, in the level of transportation costs? Could the addition of "new" territories to the international network be regarded as "independent" or is it simply the outcome of a fall of transportation costs in international trade? This is obviously just a matter of the analytical framework; it should not change the essence of the prediction of the performance of international trade. Be it as it may, such "new" additions may be noted. The opening of vast tracts of Brazil would be an obvious case. Parts of South and Southeast Asia may also belong in this category.

Given that during the period at hand incomes — aggregate and per-capita — increased dramatically, in what direction should such increase affect the foreign trade ratio? For quite a while a conventional expectation seemed to be the so-called "Sombart's Law".[18] The law was not primarily an empirical inference, but rather an a-priori prediction. It stated that as an economy industrializes, the share of foreign trade in its total economic

---

[18] The original statement of the "law" may be found in Sombart (1913). A clear exposition of the "law", providing additional a-priori justification of it (and supported by some empirical research relevant to that period) is provided in Deutsch and Eckstein (1961) (upon which our own reference to Sombart is based).

activity should fall. Hence, given that growth and industrialization have been almost universal, the foreign trade ratio should be expected to fall in most countries and in the world as a whole — an "anti-globalization" trend. "Sombart's Law" is, most probably, of doubtful (general) validity on a-priori ground. First, as Kuznets indicated (supported by his findings), it could not apply to economies at early stages of industrialization. There, as was pointed out earlier, a process of specialization, moving out of autarchy, implying (almost by definition) an increased role of trade in general and, presumably, of foreign trade as part of it. But even beyond it, the "Law" is based on the following presumptions: Trade among nations originates from differences in fundamental economic circumstances and structures. It depends, first and most, on differences in (natural) availability of resources. As the economies industrialize, they become more similar to each other. Hence, there is smaller scope for specialization and trade among them. The basic presumption here is that specialization and trade depend primarily on "natural" differences, and that they involve primarily the exchange of goods produced by highly-industrialized economies with natural-resources based goods produced by less-industrialized economies. It is commonly accepted today, on the other hand, that this pattern (the "Heckscher-Ohlin" type of trade) reflects only part of world trade, and probably its minor part, in recent years, whereas much of present-day world trade involves the exchange of basically similar (mostly industrialized) goods.[19] Moreover, this has been partly the case not only for recent decades, but even at the beginning of the period surveyed — by the middle, that is, of the 20th century.[20] Hence, an opposite a-priori expectation should be suggested, that is: the further potential trade partners industrialize and raise their incomes, the larger the scope of trade between them.

---

[19] This presumption is strongly reinforced, if trade in energy products (oil and gas) is excluded from the observation.

[20] The share of primary goods vs. finished and semi-finished goods in aggregate world trade fell from about two-thirds at the turn of the 20th century to about a half by the late 1950s. At the latter period, the majority of world trade was conducted by the highly industrialized countries among themselves (the UK, a major player in world trade prior to World War II, being an exception). See Michaely, (1968). The bibliography in this paper may also be consulted for works dealing with economic growth and foreign trade prior to the mid-19th century.

The process of industrialization should also be relevant in a different manner. As has just been mentioned, trade must increase when a country's economic activity turns from the contribution of small, autarchic units to specialization. While during the 19th century economies (primarily Europe) went through the process of industrialization one by one, no such general trend was apparent during the second half of the 20th century — at least not among economies which have counted for the large majority of the world's income and trade. On this score alone, a (presumably important) factor which participated in the increase of the foreign trade ratio during the 19th century was largely missing in the recent half century.

We recall that the regression analysis performed in the preceding section has shown a very weak relationship (and, if at all, negative) between the increase of the FTR and the initial income level of countries. Indeed, as we have just seen, this is also true for the smaller subset of countries covered in Table 2.3 when current-prices estimates are made; by these, the typical behavior of the FTR is similar for the high-income countries and the rest. But as we have just seen, this is no longer true when the impact of the relative price decline of trade is removed; estimated at constant prices, the FTR has increased dramatically more in the group of high-income (presumably; by and large, industrial) countries than in the rest. This stands in stark contrast to the prediction of "Sombart's Law"; it is firmly established, by the findings of this analysis, that in high income countries which were originally industrialized, the process of further economic growth has been accompanied by a particularly large increase of their FTRs — in other words, to strong intensification of the role of trade in their economies. This may reasonably be explained by the changing structure of world trade from the "classical" exchange of primary goods for manufactures to mostly trade in manufactures. But such presumption about causality would need further empirical verification.

Another element is the impact of size. Again, it is well established, and for obvious reasons, that, ceteris paribus, a small economy would tend to trade more with the world than a large economy. Presumably, then, as countries become larger in the economic sense, as they mostly have, with the increased income over the last century, they should tend to be less engaged in foreign trade. But such a proposition escapes an important distinction; as Kuznets (1965) argued and established, a tendency which applies, in the case at hand, to <u>cross-section</u> comparisons is <u>not</u> revealed in comparisons over time. That is, it is <u>not</u> found that as an economy expands, its foreign trade ratio tends to fall. Hence, the general economic growth over the last half century should not, on this score, lead to a relative contraction of foreign trade.

Still another consideration, applying mostly to more developed economies, is what may be regarded as <u>reversed-industrialization</u>. It is, once more, well established that beyond some level of economic advancement, the share of <u>tradable activities</u> in total economic output tends to <u>fall</u>. This is the other side of the coin of the expanding role of services (to a large extent government services) which, in a general way, are less tradable than goods. On this score, thus, trade and the FTR should tend to fall. While the presumed impact of this factor should indeed appear in our recorded investigation, a note should be mentioned. It is generally presumed that services as a whole (public services are a notable exception) have become, over the last century — both due to changes in their nature and to fall of transfer costs — more tradable (and traded globally). Hence, had an empirical investigation included trade in services (unlike the nature of our study), the FTR should appear to rise more (or fall less) than the FTR which includes only trade in goods is estimated.[21]

In view of these <u>a-priori</u> considerations, what lessons may the study of actual performance of the size of trade teach us?

---

[21] During the period addressed in the study, a remarkable increase has taken place in the size of long and medium-term (as well as short-term) international capital flows. Might this development have participated in expanding trade in goods and services, that is, the size of global <u>trade</u> related to the size of global capital flows? This is an intriguing question, presumably of some significance. Unfortunately, we do not have a ready-made answer to it. The "transfer mechanism", through which a capital outflow leads to a surplus on current account (and its opposite movements in the capital-receiving country), has been recognized for ages. Through changes in incomes and relative prices (the real exchange rate), an export surplus of goods and services should be created in the capital exporting country; exports should increase, and imports fall (and the opposite in the capital-importing country). But what should happen to the <u>combined size</u> of exports and imports, i.e., to the size of international trade and the level of the foreign trade ratio? To our knowledge, no <u>a-priori</u> analysis of this issue is available. An <u>empirical</u> investigation should be feasible, but we are not aware of its existence either.

First, whether due to one set of economic circumstance or another, we realize that in fact the level of the FTR did increase to an impressive degree. This was true for almost all countries and for practically any sub-periods during the last half century. May we draw from this progress any conclusion about the sources leading to it? Without an entirely separate research — much beyond the scope of the present one — no such answer is provided here. But we may suggest some general observations. First, this is obviously not a novelty; a predominant factor must have been the drastic change of the regime of trade policies, from highly restrictive policies to a world of almost free trade. But attention should be paid to the following observation. Let us ignore the major fluctuations of trade regimes during the 20th century and compare the early 21st century and the century's inception (i.e., the eve of WWI). These are similar periods, with global trade being almost free in both. Yet, the FTR increased remarkably over the century in between. Hence, other elements than the trade regime must have participated in leading to the expansion of trade. This (admittedly, tentative) inference may be supported by the fact that, with fluctuations, the expansion of trade did <u>not</u> slow down in more recent decades, by which time the trade liberalization process had been largely exhausted.

Of the other elements, as Kuznets indicated, the nature of technological progress must be prominent. But on the present occasion, a bias of this development towards trade should be viewed as an <u>inference</u>, rather than as being explicit. We may reasonably assume that technological change has led to a relative decline of <u>transportation costs</u>.[22] But we do not know, without further investigation, whether such change was biased towards foreign rather than domestic trade.[23] One change which may nevertheless be assumed to have indeed been so biased is the drastic fall of costs of transportation by <u>air</u>, which must be more relevant to foreign than to

---

[22] Findlay and O'Rourke (2007, pp. 503–505) argue, based on several pieces of evidence — mainly studies by Hummels — that technological progress has <u>not</u> led to reduction of transportation costs; instead, these have remained, with fluctuations, roughly stable over the last half century. They assign this contrast to relative increases of some major inputs in transport costs, such as oil, and to government and private interference in the market.

[23] An important element must have been the easing of transportation and communication costs in the trade of <u>services</u>, but this trade is not covered in the present study.

domestic trade, at least in the large majority of countries whose territorial size is much less than approaching that of a continent.[24]

Referring again to the a-priori considerations discussed earlier, the issue of the relationship of the trade ratio to the process of growth is clearly decided by the experience of the last half century; the so-called "Sombart's law", of much influence at the dawn of the 20th century, is resolutely refuted. During a period of almost unequally rapid growth of income and product the trade ratio increased dramatically rather than falling, as the "law" would predict. Moreover, whereas the major trade expansion of the 19th century accompanied a strong process of industrial revolution, this is not true for the modern period under consideration. During this era, an increased weight must be assigned to the changing composition of trade, from the exchange of primary goods for manufactures to the predominance of trade in the latter. Much of this is reflected in the increased importance of intra-industry — particularly intra-product — trade, which will be investigated in a later chapter of this book. It should be noted, in this context, that a less-impressive relative expansion of trade took place in Europe, the trade of whose countries had consisted even earlier of the exchange of manufactured goods among each other.

Has the rate of expansion of trade been related to the initial level of a country's per capita income? The a-priori considerations do not prove a clear-cut answer; elements relevant to this issue point out in contradicting directions. Indeed, the findings of the study do not provide a definite answer either. The relationship of trade expansion and initial income levels appears to be negative; but this relationship is weak enough to deny a strong inference. On this score, too, Europe deserves special attention. Europe is clearly the part of the world in which the trade share was high all throughout, including the start of the half-century analyzed here; the findings of this study indicate that trade expansion is inversely related to the size of trade at the initial point. In other words, the higher the trade

---

[24] Note, though, the paradox: though costs of transporting by air fell dramatically, these costs by themselves must lead to an increase of the level of aggregate costs of transportation; the latter is a weighted average, and the large increase of the share of transportation by air, which is normally much more expensive than other modes of transportation, leads to an increase of this average.

share a country starts with, the <u>slower</u> the expansion of trade in following years. Hence, the lower the initial trade ratio, the larger the scope for trade expansion. The most important instance that falls within this rule is the USA, whose trade ratio was traditionally very low and increased over the period by a factor of about 4.5, in comparison with an (unweighted) average for the universe of countries which just about doubled.

Finally, it should be noted that the increase of (economic) <u>size</u> of most of the participants in global trade has <u>not</u> inhibited the trade expansion. As Kuznets emphasized (1964), the strong negative correlation, which is always found in <u>cross-sectional</u> studies, between the size of an economy and the level of its foreign trade ratio does <u>not</u> hold when comparisons over time are investigated. There is no evidence that as an economy's size grows its foreign trade ratio should shrink.

A final note: attention should be paid not just to the <u>causes</u> of changes of the trade ratio but to their <u>estimation</u>. It has long been recognized that as an economy advances, the price of its tradable (and traded) goods, relative to non-tradable and to the aggregate of national income and product, tends to <u>fall</u>.[25] But the available estimates of changes of FTRs at constant prices are commonly very partial in coverage, either in time or space. In the present study, we provide a rather inclusive estimate of this trend for the half century under consideration. It is found that the presumed relative-sectoral price fall has indeed, taken place, strongly and consistently. As a result, when changes in the foreign trade ratio are estimated at <u>constant</u> rather than current prices, the trade expansion appears to have been even much more dramatic. And, it should be noted, it is the constant-prices estimate which is relevant to issues such as the share of trade in the use of an economy's resources. The need to add estimates made at constant, in addition to current-prices estimates is thus clearly indicated by the findings of the present study.

---

[25] This recognition is, <u>inter-alia</u>, the source of establishing estimates of the purchasing-party and of the divergence of this rate from the conventional (i.e., market) exchange rate.

Chapter 3

Trade Structure and Trade Performance

The Issue

Some countries have performed well in world trade, increasing their shares in the global trade; others have performed poorly. Is there any relationship of such performance to the <u>initial</u> structure of each country's trade? Intuitively, the answer should be positive, though only the <u>sign</u>, not the size, may be guessed. This potential relationship will be explored in the present chapter (as in earlier parts, the study will be confined to the structure and performance of exports).

Some goods, or sectors, have increased their shares in world trade (imports, or exports — notionally the two are equal) over the period surveyed. Call these "advancing" sectors. Others, to the contrary, have realized declines of their shares in the total; call these "lagging" sectors. Countries also differ in their export structures: some specialize (initially) in sectors which prove to be "advancing", whereas others specialize in "lagging" sectors. It should be expected, a-priori, that the former countries should have some advantage — that is, that they possess an attribute which should contribute to a relative expansion of their exports — while members of the other category of countries should suffer from a disadvantage, in view of a factor which should contribute to a decline of their relative shares in global trade.

In a similar manner, the <u>geographic</u> structure of a country's trade should be of some consequence. Some countries have realized an increase of their shares (imports, in this case) in world trade; others have witnessed declines of their shares. As an exporter, each country "specializes" in some customer countries; that is, in comparison with other exporters it concentrates in some customers at the expense of others. As before, it may be expected that a country whose exports tend (initially) to be directed more to customer countries whose shares in world exports expanded should benefit from such geographic specialization, the latter should contribute to a relative expansion of the share of the exporting country, and vice versa for a country which happens to direct its exports more to customers whose shares in world imports have declined.

We shall devise the appropriate indices — separately for the commodity and geographic structures of imports — to estimate quantitatively the impact of these trade structures. The following section will address the commodity structure. Next, in Section 3, we shall explore the impact of the geographic structure.

The Impact of Commodity Structure

We start by constructing an appropriate index to estimate the impact of the attribute at hand:

Let

X_{ij} = Exports of good i by country j
$X_{.j}$ = Aggregate exports of country j
X_{iw} = Aggregate world exports of good i
$X_{.w}$ = Total world exports
$0,1$ = Starting (base) and end periods

Then:

$$\left(\frac{X_{.j}}{X_{.w}}\right)^0 \Big/ \left(\frac{X_{.j}}{X_{.w}}\right)^1 = \text{shares of country j in world exports in periods 0,1}$$

$$\left(\frac{X_{iw}}{X_{.w}}\right)^0 \Big/ \left(\frac{X_{iw}}{X_{.w}}\right)^1 = \text{shares of good i in total world exports in periods 0,1}$$

$$\left(\frac{X_{ij}}{X_{.j}}\right)^1 = \text{shares of good i in country j's aggregate exports}$$

Define: EC_j^1 = "Predicted" share of country j in world exports in period 1.

$$EC_j^1 = \sum_i \left[\left(\frac{X_{ij}}{X_{.j}} \right)^0 * \left(\frac{X_{iw}}{X_{.w}} \right)^1 \right]$$

This is a weighted average expected on the assumption that the shares of goods in country j's exports remain unchanged, but the world exports are those of the end rather than of the base period.

Define further:

(1) $\left(\frac{X_j}{X_w} \right)^1$ is the <u>actual</u> share of country j in world exports in period 1; and

(2) $RA_j^1 = \left(\frac{X_j}{X_w} \right)^1 / EC_j^1 = $ The ratio of the actual to the "predicted" shares of country.

The ratio (2) thus shows the extent by which the actual share of the country's exports exceeds (if this ratio is above unity) or falls short of (if below unity) the predicted share.

This system thus estimates to what extent the change in a country's export share is "due" (in an accounting sense) to the performance of its export goods in world trade. The larger the relative increases in world exports of the goods in which the country specializes, the more positive the change of the country's share in world trade.[1]

We start with the first building block in this construct, namely the changes of relative shares, over the period, of individual goods in total world exports. Table 3.1 presents these shares, for goods classified by the

---

[1] One limitation of this line of exploration should be noted. It refers, by definition, only to trade in goods that already <u>existed</u> at the base period (in our case, 1965) and disregards those that came into existence in later years, for which records are available for the end year (2010). That is, it does <u>not</u> refer to the manner in which a country's exports have only reacted to the appearance of 'new' goods. In our specific estimates, close to a half (by value) of aggregate world exports in 2010 consisted of goods which had not appeared at all in the records of 1965.

Table 3.1:   Sectoral performance in trade

SITC (1)	Description (2)	$\left(\dfrac{X_{iw}}{X_{.w}}\right)^{1965}$ (3)	$\left(\dfrac{X_{iw}}{X_{.w}}\right)^{2010}$ (4)	(4)/(3) (Ratio) (5)
54	Medicinal and Pharmaceutical	0.19	4.54	23.85
57	Plastics in primary form	0.08	1.37	17.81
01	Meat and products	0.08	0.70	9.04
56	Fertilizers	0.13	0.48	3.57
58	Plastic in non-primary form	0.43	1.34	3.08
55	Essential oils, perfume, toilet	0.14	0.42	3.05
09	Miscellaneous edible products	0.29	0.63	2.17
82	Furniture	0.77	1.56	2.04
08	Feeding stuff for animals	0.31	0.62	1.97
66	Non-metabolic mineral manufactures	1.52	2.40	1.58
07	Coffee, tea, cocoa, spices	0.24	0.38	1.57
06	Sugared preparations, honey	0.18	0.26	1.45
62	Rubber manufactures	0.44	0.63	1.44
61	Leather and manufactures	0.31	0.42	1.36
28	Metal ores and scrap	1.18	1.55	1.32
11	Beverages	0.67	0.77	1.16
85	Footwear	0.97	1.09	1.12
89	Miscellaneous manufactures	4.75	5.05	1.06
51	Organic chemicals	3.98	4.21	1.05
59	Chemical material and products	1.66	1.71	1.03
03	Fish	0.61	0.60	0.97
64	Paper and paperboard	1.59	1.53	0.96
84	Apparel and clothing	3.59	3.43	0.96
05	Vegetables and fruits	1.80	1.54	0.85
72	Specialized machinery	6.14	4.94	0.80
69	Manufactures of metals, b. & c.	4.20	3.30	0.79
68	Non-ferrous metals	4.76	3.54	0.74
43	Animal or vegetable fats, oils	0.09	0.07	0.71

Table 3.1:   (Continued)

SITC (1)	Description (2)	$\left(\dfrac{X_{iw}}{X_{.w}}\right)^{1965}$ (3)	$\left(\dfrac{X_{iw}}{X_{.w}}\right)^{2010}$ (4)	(4)/(3) (Ratio) (5)
61	Leather and manufactures	0.29	0.61	0.67
04	Cereals and preparations	0.96	0.61	0.64
33	Petroleum products	5.69	3.44	0.60
53	Dying and its materials	1.13	0.66	0.58
63	Cork and wood manufactures	0.87	0.45	52
67	Iron and steel	8.18	4.20	51
29	Crude animal and vegetable materials	0.87	0.42	0.48
73	Metal working machinery	3.99	1.90	48
27	Crude fertilizers	0.64	0.25	0.39
86	Central instruments, clocks	3.84	1.28	0.33
71	Power-generating machinery	16.82	5.24	31
65	Textile yarn and fabrics	9.07	2.72	0.30
25	Pulp and paper	1.73	0.44	0.25
26	Textile fibers	1.03	0.23	0.22
24	Cork and wood	2.11	0.34	0.16
41	Animal oils and fats	0.42	0.05	0.11

2-digit SITC. Column (3) of the table shows these shares in the base year (1965), whereas column (4) records the changes in these shares over the period. The goods are presented by descending order of this ratio. Several observations are suggested by this table.

First, the changes in the relative shares have indeed been substantial. Even disregarding extreme cases (such as a ratio of 23.9 for good 54, or of 0.11 for good 41), the dispersion of the ratios is high.[2] For only a few goods are the ratios at hand close to unity (say, between 0.8 and 1.2 for only 10 goods out of the total of 45). Thus, the initial commodity structure

---

[2]As might be expected, particularly high ratios are recorded for goods whose initial shares were relatively small.

of a country's exports does look, <u>a-priori</u>, to be of consequence for its future export performance.

Second, no clear-cut pattern may be distinguished for these changes. Of particular interest may be the distinction between primary and manufactured goods. It is often taken for granted that the relative shares of primary goods have declined, and those of manufactured goods increased. Such a pattern does <u>not</u> suggest itself by the recordings of Table 3.1. For 19 categories of primary goods, the ratio at hand is above unity for 8, and below it for 10, not much of a difference. In both groups of countries, ratios above and below unity are practical equal. The median values of the ratios are 0.97 for primary goods, and 1.03 for manufactures — practically equal values, around the ratio of unity. On this evidence, thus, primary goods and manufactures have performed about equally well over the period.[3] Just on this basis, thus, there is no room to assume, <u>a-priori</u>, that changes in relative shares of goods in world trade have worked for or against the trade performance of countries specializing (initially) in primary goods versus manufactures.

We now move to the main object of our analysis, namely, estimating the impact of initial structure of a country's exports on its future export performance.

This is done through the findings recorded in Table 3.2. Column (1) of the table presents the countries (for which appropriate data are available) in descending order of the "predicted ratio". Column (2) records the "predicted" share of a country's exports in the world's total at the end period (2010), based on its export structure in the base period (1965) and the performance of individual goods in aggregate world exports, as it has just been recorded in Table 3.1. Next, column (3) of the table presents the <u>actual</u> share of the country's exports in global exports by the end period (2010). Finally, column (4) shows the ratio of column (3) to column (2); that is, the ratio of actual to "predicted" changes of the country shares at the end of the period.

---

[3] All these records of performance must represent, <u>inter alia</u>, changes in <u>relative prices</u> of goods. We have made no attempt here to separate out this factor. It should also be noted that all observations are <u>unweighted</u>, so that no conclusions for <u>aggregated</u> groups necessarily follow from the suggested inferences.

Table 3.2:   Changes of countries' export shares, based on commodity structure

Country (1)	Predicted Ratio (2)	Actual Ratio (3)	Ratio (3)/(2) (4)	Dissimilarity Index (5)
India	9.04			0.566
Honduras	7.18	3.22	0.45	0.752
Nicaragua	6.84	1.18	0.17	0.872
Costa Rica	5.83	8.76	1.50	0.550
Guatemala	3.89	3.40	0.88	0.636
Iceland	1.88	4.86	2.59	0.852
Argentina	1.35	3.26	2.42	0.671
Ghana	1.33	1.11	0.84	0.904
Burundi	1.26	0.89	0.71	0.930
Madagascar	1.24	0.27	0.22	0.751
Australia	1.18	1.99	1.69	0.708
Philippines	1.10	1.16	1.05	0.593
New Zealand	1.04	1.95	1.87	0.679
El Salvador	1.04	1.62	1.56	0.595
Sri Lanka	1.02	1.61	1.58	0.798
Nigeria	0.98	17.91	18.21	0.939
Thailand	0.96	20.09	21.01	0.461
Hungary	0.96	11.70	12.24	0.272
Senegal	0.94	0.76	0.80	0.590
Ireland	0.94	9.67	10.26	0.534
Morocco	0.93	8.11	0.87	0.741
Spain	0.93	2.42	2.61	0.324
Iran	0.91	4.89	5.27	0.782
Bolivia	0.91	1.52	0.17	0.924
Tunisia	0.88	4.43	5.01	0.585
Togo	0.88	2.11	0.24	0.722
Jordan	0.87	0.88	7.95	0.586
Afghanistan	0.86	0.06	0.07	0.585

(Continued)

Table 3.2:   (*Continued*)

Country (1)	Predicted Ratio (2)	Actual Ratio (3)	Ratio (3)/(2) (4)	Dissimilarity Index (5)
Norway	0.86	0.79	0.91	0.695
China – Hong Kong	0.86	2.38	2.77	0.121
Turkey	0.82	3.90	4.75	0.521
Chile	0.81	0.82	1.01	0.831
Netherlands	0.81	0.71	0.88	0.196
Peru	0.81	1.00	1.24	0.807
Denmark	0.80	0.60	0.75	0.321
Israel	0.80	3.23	4.04	0.465
Burkina Faso	0.78	6.71	8.41	0.945
Greece	0.77	0.98	1.26	0.489
Mexico	0.76	4.71	6.09	421
France	0.75	0.46	0.60	0.267
Portugal	0.75	0.63	0.85	0.388
Malaysia	0.74	7.84	10.48	0.343
Malta	0.74	1.08	1.45	0.454
Cambodia	0.74	7.53	10.19	0.907
Singapore	0.74	5.19	7.05	0.214
UK	0.73	0.29	0.39	0.234
Austria	0.73	0.73	1.01	0.266
Italy	0.72	0.58	0.80	0.465
Sudan	0.71	12.38	17.30	
Belgium	0.71			0.172
Germany	0.70	0.59	0.84	0.237
Switzerland	0.70	0.59	0.84	0.368
Cameroon	0.70	0.38	0.54	0.693
Rep. of Korea	0.70	18.70	20.83	0.486
Canada	0.70	0.78	1.12	0.392
Benin	0.69	2.26	3.29	0.562

Table 3.2: (*Continued*)

Country (1)	Predicted Ratio (2)	Actual Ratio (3)	Ratio (3)/(2) (4)	Dissimilarity Index (5)
Japan	0.68	0.69	1.02	0.599
USA	0.68	5.54	0.82	0.362
Mali	0.62	42.67	68.50	0.454
Colombia	0.62	1.24	1.99	0.737
Brazil	0.61	3.38	5.51	0.620
Venezuela	0.61	0.54	0.90	0.951
Libya	0.60	0.08	0.14	0.977
Ecuador	0.57	5.55	9.78	0.818
Niger	0.54	2.64	4.89	0.826
Sweden	0.54	0.37	0.69	0.291
Egypt	0.51	1.03	2.04	0.584
Suriname	0.40	0.12	0.24	0.886
Finland	0.47	0.47	1.01	0.477
Mauritania	0.40	19.59	48.38	0.990
Myanmar	0.32	1.10	3.49	0.990
Cent. African Rep.	0.31	0.39	1.26	0.961
Côte d'Ivoire	0.30	0.36	1.21	0.746
Paraguay	0.26	1.04	4.07	0.924
Congo	0.20	1.05	5.26	0.650

Several inferences may be suggested. First, looking at column (2), an extremely large variance is recorded. Conceptually, the overall change in the world's share in world trade being zero, the average ratio of the changes in shares of individual countries should be around unity.

The mean value of the levels recorded in Column (2) is indeed close to it — it is 1.10, slightly higher than unity, granting (as an unweighted measure) undue weights to several exceptional observations. The median level recorded — 0.78 — is somewhat below unity, but still in its proximity. What stands out, however, is the large degree of dispersion of the recorded values, even should extreme cases be overlooked. Excluding, say, the highest five and the lowest five values, the recorded indices still range from a low of 0.40 to a high of 1.88. This dispersion would indicate that, by itself, the initial commodity structure of a country's exports should indeed play a significant role in affecting the future performance of these exports.

Second, we ask whether countries which performed "well" or "poorly", in terms of "predicted" export shares, share some common attributes. Specifically, we ask whether more or less advanced countries, in terms of income levels (and, presumably, levels of industrialization) "perform" better or worse. We find that the less-developed countries have some advantage, but the evidence is weak enough to deny any clear-cut conclusions. The median of the recorded levels of the index is 0.744 for the advanced group (a total of 31 members), and 0.822 for the LDC's (44 members). This may be somewhat counterintuitive; conventional wisdom would probably suggest that initial export structures would grant some advantage to advanced countries. But this finding is consistent with our earlier inference that primary goods and manufactures performed about equally well in terms of their changes over the period in shares in aggregate world trade.

We have just suggested that the initial structure of exports must have a "significant" role in affecting the future performance of exports. Unfortunately, we are not aware of, nor can we devise, an index which would convey a measurable extent of such role and must adopt therefore some indications which convey impressions rather than firm inferences. For one such indication, Column (3) in Table 3.2 records the ratio of the actual change of a country's export share (from 1965 to 2010) to the "expected" share. A ratio of unity would show that in a statistical sense, the change of the "expected" share fully explains the performance of exports over the period. Needless to say, this may be entirely a coincidence; the ratio at hand may be around unity as a result of many (conflicting) factors that determined export performance during the period. Nevertheless, the levels recorded in Column (3) may be of some meaning.

We observe that the median value of the estimates recorded in column (3) is 1.45 — not unity, but still in the proximity of this level. What is remarkable, however, is that there is no clustering around this value.

To the contrary, Column (3) presents a very large degree of dispersion. Thus, for instance, even excluding the five highest and the five lowest observations on record, the ratios would range from as low as 0.24 to as high as 17.30. To suggest another way of looking at it, of the 76 observations roughly a half — 40 altogether — are either above the level of 2.00 (31 observations) or below 0.60 (9 observations). This record would suggest, again, that the impact of initial commodity structures on future export performance could not be overwhelming.

The reasons for deviation of the actual from the "predicted" performance of exports are, of course, numerous; they amount to an indication of factors which determine export performance, primarily, presumably, sets of policies overall macro-economic, exchange rate, commercial, or industry-specific policies.[4] The analysis of such factors, or even their recording, is clearly beyond the scope of the present study. Here, we are addressing attributes of <u>structures</u> of trade, or changes thereof in their relationship to export performance. This leads us to the observation of <u>changes</u> of structure — in distinction from <u>initial</u> levels — as having a potential relationship to export performance. Specifically, we pose the question: is there a relationship between the deviation of the actual from the predicted export performance to the <u>changes</u> of export commodity structure over the period investigated (1965 to 2010)?

In Table 3.2, the last Column (5) presents the index of dissimilarity of trade structures in the initial (1965) and final (2010) ends of the period; that is, the degree to which the structure at the end period differs from that of the initial one (for definition of the index, see the last section of this chapter).

Before turning to the investigation of the relationship at hand, it is worth indicating one glaring observation of an attribute of the level of the dissimilarity index; namely, its relationship to the overall level of a country's development. Even a superficial look at the data of Column (4) should reveal that particularly high levels of this index tend to be recorded for low-income countries; and, vice versa, particularly low indices are recorded

---

[4] Note, though, that one such factor — changes in relative international price of goods — is <u>not</u> a separate one; it is implicitly included in the estimates at hand which are based on values reordered at <u>current</u> prices.

for high-income countries. We test this association more formally by separating the universe of countries addressed in the table into two groups: "advanced countries" and "low income" countries (the latter include some middle-income countries).[5] Altogether, 25 (out of the universe of 75) countries are classified into the "advanced" group, and 50 countries into the "low-income" group. The <u>median</u> level of the index of dissimilarity is 0.388 for the first ("advanced") group 8; whereas for the "low-income" group it is as high as 0.693. To illustrate the radical difference between the two groups, we observe that in only three of the "advanced" countries (of a total of 25) are the levels of the index <u>higher</u> than the median (0.693) for the low-income group whereas for 46 (out of 50) low-income countries the recorded level of the index is higher than the median (0.388) for the group of "advanced" countries. It almost appears as if the two groups are — for the attribute at hand — two separate populations.

Clearly, the commodity structure of the exports of low-income countries tended to change over the period covered, much more radically than the structure of exports of the high-income countries. A reasonable hypothesis for the origin of this striking difference is the following. To start with — i.e., at the base period — exports of low-income countries tended to be much more concentrated than those of high-income countries; any diversification of structure must have led to a high level of dissimilarity of export structures between the start and the end points of observation. High-income economies, with much more diversified exports at the start period, could not expect much further diversification of export structure over the period; hence, no radical differences in structures between the two ends might be expected. But we shall further explore this hypothesis in Chapter 4 when we focus on the issue of trade diversification.

We turn now to the investigation of the possible relationship between export performance over time and dissimilarity of export structure. We perform this through observing the correlation of the two with each other. The (Spearman) rank correlation of the two — Columns (3) and (4) of Table 3.2 — is found to be –0.301. It is high enough to indicate that some

---

[5] The "advanced" group includes Australia, Austria, Belgium, Canada, Denmark, Finland, France, Germany, Greece, Iceland, Ireland, Israel, Italy, Japan, Korea Rep., Netherlands, New Zealand, Norway, Portugal, Singapore, Spain, Sweden, Switzerland, UK, and USA.

relationship <u>does</u> exist, but the negative sign of the coefficient seems a bit of a surprise. Intuitively, one would probably expect that a changing commodity structure over time should encourage the growth of exports. It is possible that this negative relationship is due to the fact, just observed, that dissimilarity over time of export structures tends to be stronger among low-income countries and that these, in turn, tended to record a weaker export performance. But the latter hypothesis is tested elsewhere in this study.

The Impact of Geographic Structure

We now move to the equivalent issue, namely: to what extent should export performance over a period be affected by its <u>geographic</u> structure at the period's initial position?

To test this potential impact, we construct an index of the "predicted" change in a country's share in global exports over the period, equivalent to the one we employed earlier for "predicting" changes based on initial <u>commodity</u> structure. Thus,

Let:

X_{jk} = Exports of (home) country j to (partner) country k;
$X_{j.}$ = Aggregate exports of country j;
$M_{.k}$ = Aggregate <u>imports</u> of country k;
M_w = Aggregate world imports;
$0,1$ = Initial and end periods.

Then,

$$EG_j^1 = \Sigma_k \left[\left(\tfrac{M_k}{M_w}\right)^1 \Big/ \left(\tfrac{M_k}{M_w}\right)^0 \cdot \left(\tfrac{X_{jk}}{X_{.j}}\right)^0 \right] = \text{the ratio of country k in world}$$
imports in period 1 relative to period 0;

and $R_k^{0,1}$, the "predicted" change of j's exports from 0 to 1, is

$$ET_j^{0,1} = \sum_k r_k^{0,1} \left(\frac{X_{jk}}{X_{j.}}\right)^0$$

This is thus the change from 0 to 1 of j's exports, assuming that its structure remains unchanged but the weights of its partner countries in world imports do change.

We shall then compare this value with the actual change in j's share in world exports, $R_j^{0,1}$.

$$R_j^{0,1} = \left(\frac{X_{j.}}{X_w}\right)^1 \bigg/ \left(\frac{X_{j.}}{X_{.w}}\right)^0.$$

Table 3.3 presents the three respective magnitudes. Column (2) records the "predicted" change, $\overline{R}_j^{0,1}$; whereas column (3) presents the actual change, $R_j^{0,1}$. Column (3), then, presents the ratio of the actual to the "predicted" — $R_j^{0,1}/\overline{R}_{0,1}$.

Observation of column (1) does not suggest, at a glance, any overall regularity. In particular, the clear distinction we have observed earlier between high- and low-income countries does not appear in the present case. For the (25) high-income countries the median is 0.686, whereas for the (66) low-income countries it is 0.660, the two medians being practically equal. That is, the change over the period in the global shares of (customer) countries in world trade does not seem, in general, to favor the exports of either the high or the low-income countries.

Observation of column (3), on the other hand, showing the excess or deficiency of the actual change in export shares in comparison with the "predicted" values, does reveal a clear difference between the two country categories. The median level of this value is 0.957 for the high-income group, vis-à-vis a level of 0.733 for the low-income group. From this comparison, it appears that high-income countries tended, as a rule, to record an expansion of their exports beyond what the "neutral" assumption on which the "predicted" values are based, in comparison with the performance of low-income countries.

To test this hypothesis more rigorously, we correlated the values recorded in column (4) with the initial (1965) levels of countries' per-capita income. The (Spearman) rank correlation of the two is found to be 0.14078. It is positive: the assumed relationship does exist. But this relationship appears to be rather weak — certainly not as clear-cut as the

Table 3.3: Changes of countries' export shares, based on geographical structure

Country (1)	Predicted Ratio (2)	Actual Ratio (3)	(3)/(2) (4)
Afghanistan	0.77	0.07	0.09
Algeria	0.61	1.08	1.79
Argentina	0.81	0.73	0.90
Australia	0.79	0.86	1.10
Austria	0.61	0.98	1.59
Bahrain	0.92	1.30	1.42
Barbados	0.46	0.12	0.25
Belgium-Lux.	0.66	0.69	1.05
Benin	0.66	0.23	0.35
Bolivia	0.75	0.59	0.79
Brazil	0.80	1.38	1.71
Burkina Faso	0.57	1.12	1.95
Cambodia	1.05	2.80	2.65
Cameroon	0.64	0.19	0.30
Canada	0.87	0.45	0.52
Central Afr. Rep.	0.66	0.06	0.08
Chile	0.73	1.10	1.51
China, Hong Kong	0.93	3.03	3.26
Colombia	0.79	1.03	1.30
Congo	0.54	3.22	6.01
Costa Rica	0.74	0.75	1.01
Cyprus	0.59	0.28	0.47
Cóte d'Ivoire	0.70	0.42	0.60
Denmark	0.58	0.56	0.96
Ecuador	0.85	1.76	2.06
Egypt	0.50	0.66	1.32
El Salvador	0.77	0.38	0.49
Ethiopia	0.75	0.37	0.50
Fiji	0.58	0.23	0.40

(Continued)

Table 3.3:   (*Continued*)

Country (1)	Predicted Ratio (2)	Actual Ratio (3)	(3)/(2) (4)
Finland	0.53	0.58	1.10
Fmr. Sudan	0.84	0.73	0.87
France	0.65	0.55	0.85
Gambia	0.59	0.06	0.11
Germany	0.69	0.64	0.93
Ghana	0.60	0.19	0.32
Greece	0.59	0.82	1.40
Guatemala	0.76	0.56	0.73
Guinea	0.61	0.12	0.19
Honduras	0.78	0.35	0.44
Hungary	0.32	3.86	12.02
Iceland	0.66	0.60	0.90
India	0.63	2.08	3.28
Indonesia	1.20	2.86	2.38
Iran	1.67	0.49	0.29
Ireland	0.61	2.19	3.58
Israel	0.83	1.44	1.75
Italy	0.68	0.65	0.95
Japan	1.12	0.76	0.68
Jordan	0.41	3.91	9.47
Lebanon	0.41	0.39	0.96
Libya	0.65	0.22	0.36
Madagascar	0.70	0.14	0.20
Malawi	0.45	0.34	0.76
Malaysia	1.24	2.25	1.83
Mali	0.49	0.86	1.77
Malta	0.53	1.84	3.50
Mauritania	0.68	0.10	0.15
Mauritius	0.57	0.52	0.92
Mexico	0.90	4.71	5.25
Morocco	0.62	0.52	0.83

Table 3.3: (*Continued*)

Country (1)	Predicted Ratio (2)	Actual Ratio (3)	(3)/(2) (4)
Myanmar	1.30	1.35	1.04
Netherlands	0.59	0.81	1.38
New Zealand	0.71	0.48	0.69
Nicaragua	0.86	0.20	0.23
Niger	0.64	0.28	0.44
Nigeria	0.63	1.35	2.13
Norway	0.56	0.46	0.82
Paraguay	0.75	1.94	2.59
Peru	0.80	0.62	0.77
Philippines	1.01	0.70	0.69
Portugal	0.48	0.99	2.06
Rep. of Korea	0.93	10.67	11.46
Samoa	0.53	0.29	0.54
Senegal	0.60	0.25	0.42
Singapore	1.17	4.32	3.71
Solomon Isds.	0.67	0.27	0.40
Spain	0.68	1.97	2.89
Sri Lanka	0.51	0.47	0.92
Sweden	0.54	0.43	0.80
Switzerland	0.76	0.73	0.96
Thailand	1.25	5.22	4.19
Togo	0.59	0.23	0.39
Trinidad and Tobago	0.64	0.44	0.68
Tunisia	0.55	1.72	3.14
Turkey	0.66	3.69	5.61
USA	0.82	0.56	0.69
UK	0.69	0.42	0.70
Uruguay	0.79	0.55	0.70
Vanuatu	0.77	0.05	0.07
Venezuela	0.58	0.30	0.52
Zambia	0.69	0.14	0.20

former comparison of medians of the two income-level groups would suggest.[6]

Trade Among Similar vs. Dissimilar Countries

We now turn to a different aspect of the impact of structure on the size of trade. It is clearly related to the issue we have discussed thus far, but it deserves a separate analysis, particularly in view of the significant interest in this element apparent in recent years which is, in turn, the outcome of the current prominence of the "new" theory of the origins of trade.

A most succinct representation of the inference of this analytical development for the expected pattern of trade may be found in the Nobel lecture of Paul Krugman, one of the founders of the theory.[7] In essence, it states that present-day trade flows between countries consist to a major extent of the exchange of basically <u>similar</u> goods rather than of goods which are radically different from each other in structure. Such trade flows originate from product differentiation, economies of scale, and monopolistic competition, rather than from differences in factor contents and natural resources (the classic "Heckscher-Ohlin" trade). This change

---

[6] In addition, we may inquire to what extent the initial trade structure may affect the <u>foreign-trade ratio</u>. We may use, for this purpose, the following index:

Let:

$0,1$ = Base and end periods
X_{ij} = Exports of sector i in country j
G_{ij} = Output of sector i in country j
GDP_j = Aggregate output of country j
Then: R_{ij} = Share of exports to output in sector i = X_{ij} / G_{ij}
Finally, the "predicted" foreign trade ratio of the economy in period 1 is

$$\overline{E}_j = \sum_i \frac{R_j^1}{R_j^0} \, SH_j^0$$

This is, thus, the "predicted" FTR at the end period on the assumption that export shares in each sector remain unchanged; but the shares of output of each sector in the economy's aggregate do change from the base to the end period. While we suggest the use of this index, we have not carried it out ourselves. This is due to the paucity, at present, of appropriately classified data on output and exports.

[7] Krugman (2009).

in the nature of trade is fairly recent, resulting from the massive intensity of the process of industrialization. Hence, present-day global trade should be expected to be conducted, much more than in earlier centuries; between pairs of countries whose trade structures are similar ("similar-similar" trade, in Krugman's representation), rather than between partners which trade mostly goods basically different in nature. This is the element which we suggest to empirically test here.

To do this, we shall use two indices. First is an index of similarity of trade structures of two partners to trade flows. Once more, the exploration is confined to the structure of <u>export</u> flows.

Let,

j = "home" country; k = "partner" country
X_{ij} = Exports of good i by country j
X_{ij} = Aggregate exports of country j

And similarly for country k.

An index of <u>dissimilarity</u> of the commodity structure of the export flows of the two partners will be:

$$D_{j,k} = \frac{\sum_i \left| \dfrac{X_{ij}}{X_{.j}} - \dfrac{X_{ik}}{X_{.k}} \right|}{2}$$

Turning it into an index of <u>similarity</u>:

$$S_{jk} = 1 - D_{j,k}$$

The index will range from 0 — i.e., no single good belongs commonly to the two baskets of exports — to unity, which the index would be when the two commodity structures are identical.

In the present exploration, we shall classify goods by the 1-digit SITC; namely, exports will be classified by ten commodity groups.

Next, we use the concept of <u>intensity ratio</u> (of which an extensive use will be made later in the study).

The notation for exports is:

X_{jk} = Exports of (home) country j to (partner) country k
$X_{.j}$ = Aggregate exports of country j

For <u>imports</u>, we designate

$M_{.k}$ = Aggregate imports of (partner) k; and
M_w = Total world imports.

The intensity ratio is defined as

$$R_{j,k} = \frac{X_{jk}}{X_{.j}} \bigg/ \frac{M_{.k}}{M_w}$$

That is, the ratio shows the extent of j's exports to k in view of country k's weight in aggregate world imports. If k's share in J's exports is identical to k's share in world imports, the ratio would be unity. A ratio <u>above</u> unity indicates a <u>bias</u> in j's exports towards exporting to partner k; and, vice versa, a ratio <u>below</u> unity would indicate a <u>negative</u> bias in j's exporting to k.

We now relate these two indices to each other. A tendency towards a similar-similar trade would imply that exporting to a "similar" partner should be represented by a higher than unity intensity ratio in the home-country's exports to this specific country. It would also imply that the higher the degree of similarity, the larger is the favorable bias in trade, as represented by a higher intensity ratio. That is, our two indices should be <u>positively</u> correlated. A bias towards similar-dissimilar trade, on the other hand, should yield a <u>negative</u> correlation of the two indices.

Given the large (91) number of countries explored here, the number of <u>pairs</u> of partner countries is in the thousands. Presenting the two indices for each such pair is thus neither feasible nor would it shed much light. Instead, we just calculated the correlation between the two variables for the universe of countries. The (Spearman) rank correlation coefficient is found to be 0.153. It is <u>positive</u>, and significant at any desired level; but it is low enough to deny an overall conclusion that trade is biased towards a similar-similar pattern. An estimation for 1970 — a relatively short time after the upheaval of WWII — yields a value of 0.158, practically equal to the level of the correlation coefficient of 2010. That is, in this sense of tendency towards or away from a similar-similar trade, no change has taken place during the last four decades. Overall, thus, almost no bias towards either trade between countries with similar or dissimilar export structures is established.

Since so much of the analysis of impact of trade composition concerns trade among relatively high-income, industrialized countries, we have conducted an exploration which refers exclusively to this category of economies. We have thus isolated a group of 26 relatively advanced countries to be taken as a separate "universe"[8] and tested the relationship between the two indices at hand (index of similarity and intensity ratio) within this universe. The rank correlation (Spearman) coefficient is positive but very low, and not much difference is found between the overall correlation coefficient and the one specific to the high-income countries (in turn, 0.153 and 0.187); on this score, trade among high-income countries does <u>not</u> follow a distinctly different pattern from global trade flows. Moreover, we have conducted a similar exploration for the group of advanced countries for 1970 — almost a half century back. In this case, the rank correlation coefficient is found to be 0.083. It is a bit lower than the coefficient for 2010 (0.187), but the difference is small enough to be practically ignored. That is, examining the change over time, we find that the bias towards either similar-similar or similar-dissimilar trade has <u>not</u> changed over the (nearly) last half century — besides being, by itself, almost non-existent.[9]

---

[8] These are Australia, Austria, Belgium, Canada, Denmark, Finland, France, Germany, Greece, Iceland, Ireland, Israel, Italy, Japan, Korea Rep., Netherlands, New Zealand, Norway, Portugal, Singapore, Spain, Sweden, Switzerland, UK, and USA.

[9] In his Nobel lecture (2009), often referred to here, Paul Krugman cites extensively a study of Britain's trade pattern by R. Baldwin and P. Martin (1999). This study points out a radical change between 1910 and the 1990's. From an exchange of primary goods (imports) with manufactures (exports) in the earlier period — a dissimilar-dissimilar trade — to similar trade structures of exports and imports — similar-similar trade — in the later period. But relying on this finding to represent (at least, illustrate) the shift from dissimilar-dissimilar to similar-similar trade would not be a fortunate choice. As it happened, Britain's trade pattern prior to WWII — exchange of manufactures for primary goods — was unique.

We quote here one of the salient findings in Michaely (1968), referring to the middle of the last century.

"Underdeveloped countries ... rarely export manufactured goods. Their trade may indeed be characterized as, by and large, the export of primary goods for manufactured goods from advanced countries. But trade of high-income countries is substantially different: most of these both export and import primary goods as well as manufactures, and they buy their imports from other advanced countries as well as from undeveloped countries. Even if goods were classified in more detail than just into the two categories of primary goods and manufactures, it would be found that the composition of exports of most highly developed countries is quite similar to the composition of their imports. An important exception is the United Kingdom, which almost alone among the major trading nations exports manufactures almost exclusively, whereas it imports mainly primary goods. Because of its conspicuous place in world trade, the extreme case of Britain has often tended to be regarded as a rule, rather than an exception." (p. 109)

Annex to Chapter 3

An issue which may potentially be of some significance, related to initial trade structures, is the following: To what extent should the initial export structure have an impact on the <u>trade ratio</u>, the ratio of a country's trade (exports in our estimates) to aggregate economic activity of the country, of an economy?[10]

This potential impact may be estimated by the following index — similiar, in essence, to those used in the main text of the present chapter.

If:

    0,1   = Base and end periods
    E_j = Exports of good j
    G_i = Output of sector j
    GDP = Aggregate output of the economy.

Then:

    R_j = Share of sector j in GDP = G_j/GDP
    SH_j = Share of exports to output in sector j = E_j/G_j.

And

    ET_j^1 = Predicted trade ratio of the economy (aggregate exports to GDP)

$$ET_j^1 = \sum_j \left(\frac{R_j^1}{R_j^0} SH_j^0 \right)$$

That is, this is the "predicted" change of the country's trade ratio given an initial production structure and assuming that in each sector exports change in the same proportion as its aggregate output.

We suggest the use of this index in the hopes that this may benefit some further future research of this issue. Unfortunately, we could not follow up on it ourselves. It requires the availability of data of goods classified similarly in the records of economic activity and of

---

[10]This ratio has been the focus of the analysis in Chapter 2. The present discussion may hence be considered also in the context of that analysis.

exports — which, to our knowledge, cannot be found at present for a universe of countries.

In a broad manner the estimated change should reflect, roughly, the change of the share of "tradables" vs. "non-tradables" in the economy. But "tradables" could obviously differ much from each other in the degree of their "tradability"; hence, more than this rough classification of economic activity is of concern in such analysis.

Chapter 4

Commodity Concentration
Re-Visited

Subject Matter and Method

In the late 1950s, Michaely (1958, 1963) provided (apparently) the first systematic study of both commodity and geographic concentration of trade among nations. Since then, many explorations of this issue have been conducted but, to our knowledge, no thorough follow-up has been provided. There is room, thus, to turn back to this important aspect of global trade and observe the changes which have taken place during the last half century. We propose to do this here.

Since the differences among nations in the degree of <u>import</u> concentration were seen then — and this inference has been repeatedly reconfirmed since — the present study will address only the <u>export</u> side. The basic tool of measurement will be the Gini-Hirschman coefficient of concentration.[1]

---

[1] In his *Paternity of an Index*, published first in 1965 and reprinted in 1980, Albert O. Hirschman claimed that his work (in Hirschman, 1945) provided the origin of this tool of measurement. This is not supported by available literature. In fact, the origin of the

Let

X_{ij} = exports of good i by country j; and
$X_{.j}$ = aggregate exports of country j.

The Gini-Hirschman coefficient of commodity concentration of exports of country j is

$$GC_{jx} = 100\sqrt{\sum_i \left(\frac{X_{ij}}{X_{.j}}\right)^2}$$

In the following section, we present the basic findings of our estimates of this coefficient.

Basic Findings

As in several other occasions on this study, we have made estimates for data of (mostly) ten-year intervals, from 1965 to 2010. In order not to clog the text with space-consuming detailed presentation of the findings, the full information is presented in the Annex to this chapter. In Table 4.1, on the other hand, we present the estimates for just the beginning and final years; that is, 1965 and 2010. These provide sufficient information for the major inferences which the findings suggest.[2]

---

index would be found in Corrado Gini's contribution in 1927 (this is different, of course, from "the" Gini index, the most popular single measurement of the degree of inequality of income distribution). Hirschman has, thus, re-discovered an index which had long been in existence. Michaely first referred to it (1958) as "the Gini coefficient". Following correspondence with Hirschman, he later (1962) changed it to the "Gini-Hirschman coefficient".

[2] In Table 4.1 we list only those (70) countries for which estimates could be made for both 1965 and 2010. In future analyses in this chapter, which refer to single years, we use (with no further note) the data presented in the Annex, which cover 218 countries.

Table 4.1: Coefficients of concentration, 1965 and 2010

Country	1965 (1)	2010 (2)	Ratio (3) = (2)/(1)
Afghanistan	41.1	39.7	0.97
Argentina	35.2	18.6	0.53
Australia	34.5	28.4	0.82
Austria	15.7	11.1	0.71
Belgium-Lux	16.1	13.7	0.85
Benin	58.8	32.2	0.55
Bolivia	64.0	33.6	0.53
Brazil	46.0	19.9	0.43
Burkina Faso	64.1	65.8	1.03
Burundi	73.9	62.7	0.85
Cambodia	59.9	42.2	0.70
Cameroon	41.1	34.9	0.85
Canada	19.9	15.8	0.79
Central Afr. Rep.	59.5	49.5	0.83
Chile	68.7	42.1	0.61
Colombia	66.1	31.1	0.47
Congo	57.8	52.3	0.91
Costa Rica	50.1	19.9	0.40
Cote d'Ivoire	48.1	38.7	0.80
Denmark	19.0	13.1	0.69
Ecuador	49.5	42.3	0.86
Egypt	57.7	15.5	0.27
El Salvador	55.0	22.0	0.40
Finland	37.7	17.5	0.47
Germany	18.9	13.8	0.73
Ghana	72.6	62.1	0.54
Guatemala	53.9	17.4	0.32
Honduras	47.8	26.4	0.55

(*Continued*)

Table 4.1:   (*Continued*)

Country	1965 (1)	2010 (2)	Ratio (3) = (2)/(1)
Hong Kong	31.7	20.4	0.64
Iceland	63.7	46.8	0.74
India	25.5	18.9	0.74
Iran	70.8	42.8	0.60
Ireland	28.8	26.5	0.92
Israel	40.9	30.5	0.74
Italy	16.4	10.2	0.62
Japan	17.7	15.5	0.88
Jordan	36.1	19.1	0.53
Korea Rep.	23.6	17.0	0.72
Libya	98.5	63.1	0.64
Madagascar	37.6	19.6	0.52
Malaysia	46.3	17.5	0.38
Mali	45.3	74.8	1.65
Mexico	23.1	16.8	0.73
Morocco	36.4	17.0	0.47
Myanmar	63.2	39.2	0.62
Netherlands	14.3	18.1	1.26
New Zealand	43.8	20.9	0.48
Nicaragua	53.6	31.4	0.59
Niger	61.9	54.9	0.89
Nigeria	41.6	56.6	1.36
Norway	20.3	33.7	1.66
Pakistan	39.5	23.4	0.59
Paraguay	33.8	40.3	1.19
Peru	35.3	29.2	0.83
Philippines	38.2	33.2	0.87
Portugal	19.3	11.9	0.62
Samoa	55.3	52.7	0.96
Senegal	52.5	25.5	0.49

Table 4.1: (*Continued*)

Country	1965 (1)	2010 (2)	Ratio (3) = (2)/(1)
Sierra Leone	31.4	25.3	0.81
South Africa	23.4	13.1	0.56
Spain	64.7	26.0	0.40
Sudan	53.2	68.6	1.29
Sweden	22.5	13.6	0.61
Switzerland	21.5	22.2	1.03
Togo	47.9	30.0	0.63
Tunisia	34.2	17.8	0.52
Turkey	35.1	11.7	0.33
UK	17.1	14.8	0.88
USA	15.3	13.0	0.85
Venezuela	70.9	53.2	0.75
Median	**41.1**	**26.4**	**0.70**

Interpretation

It is immediately apparent that a radical <u>reduction</u> of the level of commodity concentration of exports has taken place over the period under consideration. We illustrate it with a few observations. The <u>median</u> level of the coefficient went down from 41.1 in 1965 to as low as 26.4 in 2010, a fall by close to a half. In 62 (out of 70) countries — close to 90 percent of this universe — the coefficient declined, against 8 instances in which it increased. In only 18 (of 70) countries was the coefficient in 1965 <u>lower</u> than the <u>median</u> of 2010; or put conversely, in only 17 countries is the level of the coefficient in 2010 <u>higher</u> than its <u>median</u> in 1965. This trend of change is thus unmistaken and very substantial.[3]

---

[3]This trend is consistent over time, but the changes nevertheless vary substantially. The median level of the coefficient (for a universe of countries very slightly different from that represented in Table 4.1) is:

1965	1970	1975	1980	1985	1990	1995	2000	2005	2010
43.8	45.0	48.9	45.3	41.6	33.8	30.3	31.9	30.3	28.4

What is similarly apparent is that the fall of the level of concentration is <u>not</u> uniform; it varies over a wide range. This is made clear by looking, in Column (3) of Table 4.1, at the ratio of the level in 2010 to that of 1965. By itself, this ratio <u>cannot</u> be given an economic meaning (for instance, stating that the level of concentration "fell by a half" means nothing beyond the statement that the coefficient fell by a half); but it does convey the extent of the change. This ratio ranges from a level not much below unity (excluding from this observation instances in which the level actually <u>increased</u>) — that is, instances with almost no change, to ratios as low as 0.27 (in Egypt) — which indicate a drastic fall of the level of concentration.

Moreover, a clear distinction appears to be between countries with initially high levels of concentration and those which initially started with low levels. In the former group, as a rule, concentration fell substantially, whereas in the latter it changed relatively little. In a sense, this is inevitable; where concentration was low to start with, there was only little room for it to fall further. Yet, it may be rewarding to attempt to reveal potential sources of the fall of concentration; that is of commonality of attributes of countries which share this development.

The first, and foremost, attribute which suggests itself is the <u>commodity structure</u> of exports. When a country specializes in exports of basic commodities — resources, heavily resource-based goods, or basic staples — it may be expected to have only a few goods in which the natural origins of goods will provide the country an advantage; hence, to have highly concentrated exports; whereas an economy which exports fabricated, heavily manufactured goods should on the other hand manifest a relatively low level of concentration. Indeed, a look at column (1) of Table 4.1 would immediately indicate — without verifying it at the moment with precision — that at the base period (1965) practically all countries with high levels of export concentration could be characterized as exporting exclusively (or at least predominantly) resource-based or staple commodities. A drastic fall in concentration may hence be expected to go hand in

---

It appears that the major fall of the level of concentration occurred between 1980 and 1995; the level moved only little prior to this period and following it. Without further detailed research, we cannot explain offhand this variation over time.

hand with a similarly drastic fall of the role of such goods in a country's aggregate exports. Similarly, the two attributes must be closely related to each other. Countries at a lower level of development (i.e., of per-capita income) demonstrate a high level of export concentration, and a particularly rapid economic development — growth of income — may hence be expected to be associated with a strong trend of fall of concentration. Still another attribute which may be looked at is that of <u>size</u> (measured by the country's <u>aggregate</u> income). In Michaely's early studies (1958, 1962) size seemed to matter among highly developed countries. Has this remained true?

We proceed now to examine the first potential relationship; i.e., of the fall of concentration with the change in export structure. This "structure" may obviously be defined and estimated in a variety of ways. To make a universal comparison feasible, we confine ourselves here, as on other occasions in this study, to a broad distinction between two classes, "resource-based" exports — categories 1 – 4 of the SITC — and "manufactures" — categories 5 – 8. The shares of the two classes of goods in each country's exports are presented in the form of the share of manufacturing, in Annex Table 2, for both the starting year of the period addressed (1965) and its end year (2010).[4]

Table 4.2 presents the measure of association — correlation coefficients — of the level of commodity concentration of exports and several explanatory variables. Since we seek no numerical impact of one variable or another, and since in any case our representations of a variable have an <u>ordinal</u> rather than a cardinal meaning, we regard the Spearman rank correlation as the proper representation of an association in the present context; but, to satisfy possible curiosity, we also represent in the table the Pearson correlation coefficient. Without specific indication in each of the separate relationships presented in the table, we note that in each of them the finding is acceptable at any desired level of confidence.

---

[4] Data are presented only for countries for which they are available for <u>both</u> ends of the period (that is, for 1965 as well as 2010). But in our further analysis, data may be used for the universe of the world's members, including countries for which data are available only for 2010.

Table 4.2: Relationship of concentration to other attributes: Correlation coefficients

Gini-Hirschman Coefficient and;		Pearson Coefficient	Spearman Coefficient
a. Share of manufactures	1965	−0.652	−0.750
	2010	−0.549	−0.615
b. Changes in Coefficient and of share of manufactures from 1965 to 2010 of Concentration		−0.104	−0.426
c. Per-capita GDP	1970	−0.425	−0.460
	2010	−0.210	−0.350
d. Aggregate GDP	1970	−0.290	−0.626
	2010	−0.252	−0.529
e. Index of Intra-Industry Trade	1965	−0.307	−0.502
	2010	−0.621	−0.741
f. Distance level of Trade	1965		
	2010	0.168	0.332

The first line (a) in the table presents the relationship we have just emphasized, of the role of the commodity structure of exports (we represent this structure, here as on other occasions in the present study, by the share of manufactures — SITC group 0 to 4 — in aggregate exports). We see that the relationship of this attribute with the level of commodity concentration is indeed strong,[5] particularly when it is represented by the Spearman rank correlation coefficient. It is somewhat weaker in 2010 than in 1965, but only to a marginal extent. That is, at present as in the past, with little change over the half century, the structure of exports appears to have a major impact on the level of concentration of a country's exports.

We go a bit further, in this direction, to ask whether the change of the level of concentration over the period is related to the change in the structure of exports. This is presented in line (b) of the table. As indicated by the Spearman coefficient, this relationship appears again to be present,

---

[5] Here as in the following observations, the sign of the correlation coefficient is negative, as should be expected.

though the relationship is weaker than when the absolute levels of the variables were examined. Thus, when looking to explain the <u>change</u> in countries' commodity concentration, the <u>change</u> in export structure appears to be meaningful.

We move now, in line (c), to observe the relationship between a country's level of commodity concentration and its degree of development, measured, as on other occasions, by its level of per-capita income. Once more, a relationship does exist. It is weaker, though, than the relationship with export structure appeared to be. It is possible that since these two attributes — export structure and income level — must be related to each other, the impact of one variable is "swallowed" by the other (we shall return soon as to this issue). Be it as it may, it does appear at the end as well as the beginning of the period that poorer countries tend to exhibit a higher level of commodity concentration than richer partners.

We move now to test a further hypothesis, concerned with the <u>size</u> of the economy. It is reasonable to expect a small economy to specialize in a smaller variety of exported goods (as well as of its production activity in general). The association of concentration with size is presented in line (d) of Table 4.2, in which (as in other explorations in the present study) economic "size" is measured by the country's aggregate GDP. (The initial year of the period is taken here as 1970 rather than 1965, due to availability of statistical resources). The presumed association is indeed revealed (once more, by the Spearman coefficient of rank correlation). The association appears to be somewhat weaker at the end of the period (2010) than at its beginning (1970), but it does not fade substantially.

An issue we have hinted to earlier is that these "explanatory variables" — export structure, per-capita GDP, and aggregate GDP — are not entirely independent from each other; to the country, they must have some relationship to each other.[6] To reveal the "net" impact of each of these, we

---

[6]A multiple regression of the three attributes on each other yields the following Spearman (rank) correlation coefficients.

	<u>1970</u>	<u>2010</u>
a. Share of manufacturing with per-capita GDP	0.573	0.240
b. Share of manufacturing with aggregate GDP	0.383	0.306
c. Per-capita GDP and aggregate GDP	0.588	0.540

Table 4.3:   A multiple regression of concentration with

		Share of Manufacturing (1)	Per-Capita GDP (2)	Aggregate GDP (3)
1970	Pearson	−0.454	−0.425	−0.290
	Spearman	−0.610	−0.460	−0.626
2010	Pearson	−0.538	−0.278	−0.252
	Spearman	−0.602	−0.394	−0.529

therefore run a multiple regression of the level of commodity concentration of exports on each of these attributes. The outcome is presented in Table 4.3, where we show both the Pearson and Spearman rank correlation coefficients; as in most of our analyses in this context, we regard the latter correlation as the more meaningful representation of the association explored in this manner. Once more without specific indication, all the findings presented in the table are acceptable at any desired level of confidence (in view of the large number of observations, i.e., if individual countries) we present in Table 4.3 the results of the analysis for both the beginning year (in this instance, 1970) and the end year (2010) of the period.

The findings suggest some clear inferences. The association of the level of concentration with each of the explanatory attributes is strong; it is so for both the start and the end year of the period under investigation. It is strongest when the variable of the share of manufactured exports in the aggregate is concerned and is almost equally strong for the relationship with aggregate GDP, the (economic) size of the country. It is weakest — though still quite strong — for the relationship with per-capita income. Apparently, this latter attribute, the degree of richness of an economy, contributes <u>less</u> to concentration than the other two attributes; this, we may recall, was indicated by the findings of the (single) regression presented in Table 4.2. It thus appears that the (economic) size of a country and its export structure are the major determinants of concentration vs. diversification of a country's trade.

We now turn to examine the possible relationship of trade concentration to two <u>patterns</u> of trade (rather than to <u>attributes</u> of trade and of the economy). First, we look at the pattern of <u>intra-industry</u> trade (which will be explored in the next chapter). It should be reasonable to assume that a country which exports just a few goods is <u>not</u> likely to concentrate its imports (and consumption) in these few goods. To the contrary, when exports are diversified over many products, it is likely that many of these will also be demanded by the country. Thus, when a country's exports are highly concentrated, it is likely to exhibit only a relatively low level of intra-industry trade, while diversified exports are likely to be accompanied by a high level of intra-industry trade.

These expectations are indeed borne out by our investigation, the outcome of which is presented in line (d) of Table 4.2. A relatively high correlation is found between the levels of export concentration and of intra-industry trade. The association is particularly strong when inferred, as it should, from the Spearman rank correlation coefficient. It is interesting — and not entirely surprising — that the association is stronger towards the end of the period (2010) than at its beginning (1965). During the half century in between, as we have inferred on earlier occasions in this study, the share of trade of highly diversified manufactured goods, which are likely to be (under given classifications) both exported and imported, grew substantially. With such a development, countries with highly concentrated exports, which are most likely <u>not</u> of the type which gives rise to intra-industry trade, stand out more than before in their low level of intra-industry trade.

Lastly, we look at the <u>distance</u> pattern of trade. Here, prior expectations are not that obvious, though some hypotheses may be suggested. It may be presumed that when a country exports only few goods, it cannot concentrate in directing its exports only to near-by countries. By this hypothesis, the distance traveled by a country's exports should be <u>positively</u> related to the level of export concentration.

This relationship is presented in line (e) in Table 4.2. For the variable of distance, we use the distance level of exports (which will be found in Chapter 7). The relationship is estimated only for the final year 2010, for which this representation of distance is available. It appears that the positive relationship does exist and that (as indicated, again, by the Spearman rank correlation) it must be at a meaningful level. A word of caution, though, should be noted; there is a close association between a country's distance level of exports and its being European. In turn, European countries are likely to be rich, export predominantly manufactured goods, and have diversified exports. It is thus possible that, partly at least, through this intermediation of "Europe", the distance level of exports reflects the impact of the earlier-analyzed attributes.

The exploration of the present chapter may thus be summed up, by way of generalization, as follows. A country with highly diversified exports may be expected to be highly developed, large (in terms of aggregate income) and an exporter of manufactured goods. It is likely to have a larger extent of intra-industry trade, and to trade relatively much with nearby countries; all of these attributes are likely to be found heavily among European countries. Highly concentrated exports, to the contrary, should characterize a less-developed country, of relatively small aggregate income, which exports predominantly primary goods, trades with relatively far-away partners, and whose trade exhibits a low level of intra-industry trade. Countries of this nature are most likely to be found in Africa and, to a lesser extent, in Latin America and some parts of Asia. The level of a country's concentration of exports thus represent to a large extent a regional geographic classification of trading countries.

Annex Table 4.1: Gini-Hirschman coefficient of commodity concentration, 1965–2010

	1965	1970	1975	1980	1985	1990	1995	2000	2005	2010	2010/1965	2010/1970
Afghanistan	41.1	35.9	35.8							39.7	0.97	1.11
Albania								29.1	26.3	21.3		
Algeria		67.8	85.4	83.2	57.1	59.5	43.0	44.2	48.3	44.2		0.65
Andorra							23.6	20.1	27.5	19.1		
Angola		41.2		74.9		92.3						
Anguilla								27.5				
Antigua and Barbuda			87.3									
Argentina	35.0	28.0	25.2	20.8	24.3	19.8	15.4	26.0	52.9	21.2	0.53	0.66
Armenia								37.0	40.1	28.4		
Aruba						39.5	35.4	40.3	82.8	58.8		
Australia	34.5	24.4	23.3	22.4	24.2	17.1	14.8	14.9	18.9	28.4	0.82	1.16
Austria	15.7	15.0	15.1	11.5	11.1	11.3	11.3	13.7	12.1	11.1	0.71	0.74
Azerbaijan								46.9	42.8	68.9		
Bahamas			68.4	69.4	71.5		38.0	20.1	35.2	27.8		
Bahrain		57.8	80.8	46.3	53.4	51.9	51.3	73.5	58.2	58.0		1.00
Bangladesh				43.9	32.7	30.7	35.1	42.2	38.9	40.5		
Barbados		45.9	52.6	34.2	49.3	33.8	23.5	22.3	25.0	24.3		0.53
Belarus								17.5	24.5	23.8		
Belgium-Luxembourg	16.1	16.6	16.1	15.5	15.9	16.0	14.2	13.3	13.9	13.7	0.85	0.82

(*Continued*)

Annex Table 4.1: *(Continued)*

	1965	1970	1975	1980	1985	1990	1995	2000	2005	2010	2010/1965	2010/1970
Belize			57.0	48.3	49.8	52.0	36.3	30.8	31.1	36.3		
Benin	58.8	39.1		47.6			54.7	69.5	59.5	32.2	0.55	0.82
Bermuda			55.2	59.2	61.2	83.5	98.5					
Bhutan									34.4	35.5		
Bolivia (Plurilateral State of)	64.0	57.6	42.6	43.1	61.5	36.7	22.2	20.5	30.5	33.6	0.53	0.58
Bosnia Herzegovina									17.3	16.7		
Botswana								82.0	75.1	68.9		
Brazil	46.0	38.4	23.9	21.5	18.0	14.7	13.9	13.2	13.4	19.9	0.43	0.52
Brunei Darussalam	95.4	94.7	79.7	69.4	69.1	65.0						
Bulgaria								16.3	15.8	15.5		
Burkina Faso	64.1	48.2	48.8	51.0			61.3	59.1	75.0	65.8	1.03	1.36
Burundi	73.9		89.0				67.9	75.6	61.9	62.7	0.85	
Cote d'Ivoire	48.1	46.5	38.8		42.1		36.8	33.7	32.4	38.7	0.80	0.83
Cabo Verde				39.7			42.9	38.4	38.0	44.2		
Cambodia	59.9	45.7						41.9	43.6	42.2	0.70	0.92
Cameroon	41.1	38.1	43.0	45.4		52.2	29.8	39.9	33.3	34.9	0.85	0.92
Canada	19.9	24.4	24.3	16.8	20.5	16.0	16.3	16.0	15.3	15.8	0.79	0.65
Cayman Isds				41.8								
Central African Rep.	59.5	51.4	41.8	45.3			44.0	65.9	44.6	49.5	0.83	0.96

Country												
Chad	78.0	72.7	66.7		43.2	43.1	34.1	31.9	35.3	42.1	0.61	0.55
Chile	68.7	77.2	58.6	45.8	35.5	14.0	12.6	12.6	13.9	13.8		
China							35.3	37.5	34.1			
China, Macao SAR			80.8	33.7	31.2	34.0				70.0		
Colombia	66.1	65.0	47.7	60.7	52.7	34.1	26.0	26.4	20.9	31.1	0.47	0.48
Comoros							78.3	88.5	87.1	69.7		
Congo	57.8	52.4	74.5	91.6	90.9		64.6			52.3	0.91	1.00
Congo, Rep. of the Dem.	54.2	68.1	56.5									
Cook Isds								92.2	43.9	69.9		
Costa Rica	50.1	44.3	38.1	34.0	41.7	32.8	28.5	26.0	17.8	19.9	0.40	0.45
Croatia							14.0	15.7	13.6	14.9		
Cuba			91.0	81.3				36.0	31.5			
Cyprus		37.7	28.5	20.3	19.9	18.0	31.9	32.3	22.9	20.2		0.54
Czech Rep.							9.6	12.2	12.8	13.7		
Czechoslovakia		21.6	21.8	18.9	17.3	12.5						
Denmark	19.0	16.9	17.0	13.4	13.0	11.6	14.3	12.4	13.0	13.1	0.69	0.77
Djibouti						57.4						
Dominica				61.8	57.2	63.7	47.8	40.0	37.8	45.1		
Dominican Rep.			68.1	48.4	33.1	33.1	23.2		23.3	18.6		
East and West Pakistan	39.5	30.7										

(Continued)

Annex Table 4.1: (*Continued*)

	1965	1970	1975	1980	1985	1990	1995	2000	2005	2010	2010/1965	2010/1970
Ecuador	49.5	53.2	62.9	58.0	64.5	51.9	31.6	36.6	42.4	42.3	0.86	0.80
Egypt	57.7	48.4	41.0	60.5	57.4	29.3	23.7	27.8	28.5	15.5	0.27	0.32
El Salvador	55.0	51.1	40.9	40.7	57.8	45.3	39.2	57.4	26.4	22.0	0.40	0.43
Eritrea								35.4				
Estonia							11.7	20.6	16.2	14.9		
Ethiopia		63.2	40.5	66.0	64.8	51.0	66.8	57.3	42.2	38.8		0.61
Faeroe Isds				49.5	60.0	60.8		51.8	51.5			
Fiji		57.2	73.0	63.3	49.7	36.8		29.7	29.4	27.0		0.47
Finland	37.5	31.6	29.6	25.4	26.5	26.7	24.4	24.7	20.8	17.5	0.47	0.55
Fmr Arab Rep. of Yemen			57.4	29.1								
Fmr Panama, Canal Zone	56.5	60.0	52.9									
Fmr Rep. of Vietnam	73.8	78.0										
Fmr Sudan	53.2	66.0	56.0	46.8	51.2		36.7	48.1	62.5	68.6	1.29	1.04
Fmr Yugoslavia	17.2	16.2	14.9	14.2	16.2	12.2						
France	13.6	15.4	16.2	11.5	11.3	11.6	10.6	11.7	12.1	12.5	0.92	0.81
French Guiana		78.4	54.6	48.3	56.8	46.3	28.6					
French Polynesia			68.1	45.3				72.3	62.4	55.6		
FS Micronesia									70.1			

Gabon	47.8	53.7	83.6	88.4				61.6	62.2			
Gambia		61.5	64.7	57.0			29.6	39.0	38.9	30.0		0.49
Georgia								20.1	23.4	24.7		
Germany	18.9	19.0	18.0	12.3	14.1	12.3	12.6	14.3	13.3	13.8	0.73	0.72
Ghana	72.6	75.8	76.0	77.9				37.5	41.5	62.1	0.86	0.82
Greece	39.2	22.4	19.9	22.1	18.3	15.1	14.0	14.6	13.0	21.2	0.54	0.95
Greenland				46.2	52.2	57.6	45.1	45.8	39.7	39.5		
Grenada				51.9	55.1	39.1	31.2	30.5	35.9			
Guadeloupe		66.7	56.1	50.2	47.1	45.4	32.1					
Guatemala	53.9	38.1	35.8	35.7	42.8	32.4	32.2	25.3	18.7	17.4	0.32	0.46
Guinea							40.2	37.7	41.3			
Guinea-Bissau		85.8	77.4				57.1	73.5				
Guyana		59.8	59.6					36.2	36.1	40.7		0.68
Haiti		43.4	33.8			29.9	35.2					
Honduras	47.8	47.3	34.0	41.3	49.2	46.3	54.4	29.0	29.5	26.4	0.55	0.56
Hong Kong	31.7	32.9	35.8	17.7	15.8	15.1	13.9	14.8	16.7	20.4	0.64	0.62
Iceland	63.6	67.8	67.0	45.3	46.0	43.3	36.2	36.1	35.8	46.8	0.74	0.69
India	25.5	20.1	20.2	17.0	19.7	19.2	19.0	19.8	17.3	18.9	0.74	0.94
Indonesia		41.5	70.2	56.2	51.6	23.7	15.6	14.7	14.7	16.8		0.40
Iran	70.8	76.1		91.7				65.3	60.1	42.8	0.60	0.56
Iraq		42.7						97.0	96.4	78.6		

(Continued)

Annex Table 4.1: *(Continued)*

	1965	1970	1975	1980	1985	1990	1995	2000	2005	2010	2010/1965	2010/1970
Ireland	28.8	22.4	21.1	17.8	19.2	18.5	18.5	22.2	22.1	26.5	0.92	1.18
Israel	40.9	35.9	36.0	33.1	27.0	31.2	31.6	35.0	40.4	30.5	0.74	0.85
Italy	16.4	17.9	17.7	12.4	12.0	11.7	11.0	10.9	10.8	10.2	0.62	0.57
Jamaica			54.7	76.6	52.5	64.4	51.3	34.0	38.9	30.8		
Japan	17.7	19.6	22.9	17.6	19.3	16.3	15.2	16.0	16.0	15.5	0.88	0.79
Jordan	36.1	33.5	43.9	32.3	35.5	36.0	21.7	14.3	17.9	19.1	0.53	0.57
Kazakhstan							22.3	39.0	47.4	51.8		
Kenya				40.7	41.6	28.0	28.0	33.8	24.9	26.8		
Kiribati			96.5	99.9	79.8	49.0	50.2		30.6	38.0		
Korea, Rep.	23.6	32.3	26.4	15.3	20.8	14.7	16.8	16.7	16.9	17.0	0.72	0.53
Kuwait		80.4	81.3	71.2		92.1	94.4	49.0				
Kyrgyzstan							18.2	36.7	30.0	41.3		
Lao People's Dem. Rep.	63.3	49.5										
Latvia							15.2	20.1	14.4	11.9		
Lebanon		18.4						16.7	14.7	19.7		1.07
Lesotho								47.1		29.3		
Liberia		73.0	75.7	56.5								
Libya	98.5	99.6	95.2	100.0	87.9	83.2				63.1	0.64	0.63
Lithuania							12.1	17.0	20.2	19.4		
Madagascar	37.6	37.2	42.5	53.4	48.0	33.6	30.5	25.2	22.6	19.6	0.52	0.53

Country												
Malawi	46.3	47.8	50.7	50.0	51.1	69.5	68.5	61.1	55.6	57.0		1.19
Malaysia		41.8	33.2	35.3	32.0	18.1	18.0	21.1	18.7	17.5	0.38	0.42
Maldives							35.5	33.2	41.0	57.9		
Mali		45.3	42.7	48.9	69.8	35.5	69.0	63.7	63.2	74.8	1.65	1.75
Malta	32.0	30.3	44.0	40.0	51.6	41.1	53.5	46.9	32.9	32.1	1.00	1.06
Martinique					55.8	54.3	50.1	51.6	47.1	47.7		
Mauritania			93.7	87.4	85.8	69.1	53.0	58.7	71.1	38.7	0.41	0.44
Mauritius			93.6	69.1	42.8	40.9	37.4	36.8	27.8	26.4		0.28
Mayotte								49.8	20.2			
Median	**35.8**	**38.0**	**46.7**	**42.0**	**35.8**	**32.4**	**30.1**	**29.5**	**29.8**	**26.9**	**0.75**	**0.75**
Mexico	23.1	18.2	21.4	61.7	55.4	27.4	14.5	15.7	16.0	16.8	0.73	0.93
Moldova. Rep.							27.0	30.1	31.2	18.8		
Mongolia								33.7	38.5			
Montenegro										41.2		
Montserrat							46.3	27.6	31.7	59.8		
Morocco	36.4	34.4	56.2	36.4	29.9	21.7	18.6	20.6	17.8	17.0	0.47	0.49
Mozambique							37.2	32.9	59.5	54.0		
Myanmar	63.2	53.3	46.7					38.4	32.9	39.2	0.62	0.74
Namibia							42.5	32.3	31.4	30.0		
Nepal		37.4	38.4	29.5	48.8	47.3		32.3	32.3	19.9		
Neth. Antilles						83.1	83.6	19.9	19.9			

(Continued)

Annex Table 4.1: *(Continued)*

	1965	1970	1975	1980	1985	1990	1995	2000	2005	2010	2010/1965	2010/1970
Neth. Antilles and Aruba	95.7	92.4	91.4	95.4	66.4						1.26	
Netherlands	14.3	14.4	17.1	18.1	18.3	12.0	10.7	19.0	17.6	18.1	1.26	1.26
New Caledonia			60.4	59.3				61.1	65.3	59.4		
New Zealand	43.8	40.6	33.1	31.2	26.0	19.3	16.9	17.3	18.7	20.9	0.48	0.52
Nicaragua	53.6	32.9	33.9	45.4	48.5	36.6	30.1	34.8	26.4	31.4	0.59	0.95
Niger	61.9	60.1	63.9	83.3			57.8	48.7	39.2	54.9	0.89	0.91
Nigeria	41.6	61.4	92.8		96.2			74.1		56.6	1.36	0.92
Niue					45.0							
Norway	20.3	21.2	26.6	35.8	38.6	37.6	30.1	38.1	36.9	33.7	1.66	1.59
Oman			99.8	96.2	33.4	66.5	58.3	60.1	53.8	45.8		
Pakistan			30.9	30.3	27.0	27.5	29.1	26.9	25.0	23.3		
Panama				38.3	37.8	33.8	30.9	25.4	33.2	25.9		
Papua New Guinea			58.6		43.3	51.2		39.5				
Paraguay	33.8	28.8	28.8	42.0	58.5	43.2	35.3	30.9	33.2	40.3	1.19	1.40
Peru	35.3	39.8	34.8	31.2	30.2	32.1	28.7	25.3	26.6	29.2	0.83	0.73
Philippines	38.2	37.4	34.6	27.1	33.8	33.8	40.3	35.1	30.8	33.2	0.87	0.89
Poland				16.1	18.7	14.4	12.5	12.3	12.4	12.1		
Portugal	19.3	18.1	18.7	15.4	15.3	16.2	15.0	14.3	12.4	11.9	0.62	0.66
Qatar			97.2			76.9	66.3	45.6	45.6	47.1		

Country												
Reunion	89.3	83.6	81.4	72.8	74.8	63.6	16.6	15.3	13.0			
Romania					18.3	16.0	26.0	30.0	32.6			
Russian Federation								41.5	42.7			
Rwanda						45.8	44.2	45.5	38.8			
Saint Kitts and Nevis												
Saint Lucia		56.1	31.7	60.0	59.5	41.0	42.4	28.8				
Saint Pierre and Miquelon			73.0									
Saint Vincent and the Grenadines			49.9			37.9	34.2	31.7	29.6			
Samoa	55.3	53.7	63.1	55.8		40.4		52.5	52.7		0.95	0.98
Sao Tome and Principe		93.2	94.6				90.8	88.9	85.0			
Saudi Arabia				77.2	75.2	56.3	60.3	57.2	60.0			
Senegal	52.5	36.2	40.7	31.9	29.9	33.2	24.7	19.5	25.5		0.49	0.71
Serbia								13.5	11.8			
Serbia and Montenegro							14.3					
Seychelles		63.9	53.8	82.5	57.9	43.6	48.9	47.6				
Sierra Leone		54.9					71.4					
Singapore	31.4	34.7	36.0	28.8	28.7	19.2	20.8	24.6	22.8	25.3	0.81	
Slovakia						13.0	16.5	14.7	17.6			
Slovenia						13.2	14.0	14.8	14.3			0.73

(Continued)

Annex Table 4.1: *(Continued)*

	1965	1970	1975	1980	1985	1990	1995	2000	2005	2010	2010/1965	2010/1970
So. African Customs Union							29.9					
Solomon Isds		66.9	53.8	60.5	44.6				79.4	56.8		0.85
Somalia		60.6	70.0	77.4								
South Africa								18.4	17.8	17.8		
Spain	23.4	17.5	16.1	13.9	16.1	14.2	16.1	15.4	14.1	13.1	0.56	0.75
Sri Lanka	64.7	60.4	53.2	42.5	38.5	32.7		28.8	26.6	26.0	0.40	0.43
State of Palestine								24.0	23.9	22.1		
Suriname	78.8					74.8	39.8	90.8	88.1	82.6	1.05	
Swaziland								26.7	38.6			
Sweden	22.5	20.7	20.9	15.6	16.1	15.8	16.5	17.1	15.1	13.6	0.61	0.66
Switzerland	21.5	20.5	20.1	15.2	14.8	13.3	13.6	15.0	19.1	22.2	1.03	1.08
Syria			70.4	65.7	55.3	40.2	56.8	69.8	45.4	32.4		
Tajikistan								57.5				
TFYR of Macedonia							17.4	19.9	20.3	18.5		
Thailand	39.9	30.9	27.7	25.0	20.1	14.2	12.9	13.4	11.9	12.1	0.30	0.39
Timor-Leste									33.2			
Togo	47.9	52.1	67.3	50.3		50.3	32.9	33.7	32.4	30.0	0.63	0.58
Tonga			70.5	50.2	44.1	47.6	55.3	65.5	61.9	38.0		
Trinidad and Tobago		70.2	62.3	65.9	57.2	48.6	32.6	33.5	32.8	31.6		0.45

Tunisia	34.2	31.5	45.9	51.4	42.6	25.2	25.1	23.3	19.8	17.8	0.52	0.56
Turkey	35.1	38.0	28.1	26.8	16.3	16.3	16.3	14.6	13.2	11.7	0.33	0.31
Turkmenistan								42.0				
Turks and Caicos Isds								25.6	37.6			
Tuvalu				80.0	97.9				55.5			
Uganda							68.1	37.1	28.3	22.1		
Ukraine								18.1	18.5	17.8		
United Arab Emirates				20.2	18.3	15.8		44.9	40.3	43.6		
United Kingdom	17.1	16.5	16.3	14.3	19.3	12.0	11.3	14.4	13.7	14.8	0.87	0.90
United Rep. of Tanzania				32.3				26.8	29.8	24.4		
Uruguay		47.3	34.7	30.1	25.3	27.3	19.6	23.1	26.4	22.8		0.48
US Virgin Isds		55.5										
USA	15.3	16.5	17.6	12.3	14.0	13.6	11.5	12.7	11.6	13.0	0.85	0.79
Vanuatu		58.3	55.0	55.0	69.0	47.1		34.5		27.8		0.48
Venezuela	70.9	68.4	71.0	70.1	57.7	79.9	41.0	48.3	49.0	53.2	0.75	0.78
Viet Nam								24.2	22.6	15.6		
Yemen							89.8	90.3	63.5	56.4		
Zambia		94.9		89.0			83.9	55.0	56.5	75.5		0.80
Zimbabwe	41.1				29.7	29.4	29.7	33.4	24.6	29.6		

Annex Table 4.2:   Share of manufactures in aggregate exports (in percentage)

Country	1965	2010	Country	1965	2010
Afghanistan	13.1	19.6	Japan	85.5	80.4
Argentina	3.0	25.3	Jordan	18.0	40.0
Australia	15.8	14.4	Korea Rep.	60.8	79.8
Austria	74.7	71.3	Libya	0.8	0.7
Belgium-Lux	75.4	47.8	Malaysia	27.0	62.3
Benin	4.0	14.5	Mali	2.6	3.8
Bolivia	6.2	9.9	Malta	50.9	58.0
Brazil	6.9	31.1	Mexico	19.6	72.6
Burkina Faso	4.3	2.9	Morocco	5.4	46.0
Burundi	5.4	4.1	Myanmar	2.9	30.7
Cameroon	22.0	8.3	Netherlands	47.4	43.1
Canada	43.3	44.4	New Zealand	2.7	21.7
Colombia	5.3	15.4	Nicaragua	8.0	5.3
Costa Rica	9.5	53.6	Niger	2.3	12.2
Cote d'Ivoire	4.7	13.0	Nigeria	6.8	6.5
Denmark	37.6	49.8	Norway	52.3	20.5
Ecuador	1.1	8.1	Paraguay	0.3	5.7
Egypt	20.0	33.0	Peru	26.9	21.7
El Salvador	13.0	66.0	Philippines	5.2	55.4
Finland	57.1	70.0	Portugal	53.6	67.5
France	62.8	61.7	Senegal	2.7	22.2
Germany	71.7	69.3	Singapore	27.1	62.1
Ghana	1.6	9.2	Spain	33.4	59.8
Guatemala	10.6	31.3	Sri Lanka	0.7	1.8
Honduras	2.9	18.7	Sweden	62.2	65.4
Hong Kong	82.7	90.8	Switzerland	71.8	52.8
Hungary	47.3	74.8	Thailand	5.6	44.6
India	46.9	55.2	Tunisia	8.6	65.7
Iran	3.8	8.3	Turkey	5.5	74.8
Ireland	24.1	25.8	UK	74.4	52.9
Israel	60.4	67.1	USA	55.1	55.2
Italy	69.6	72.1	Venezuela	0.7	3.8

Chapter 5

Intra-Industry, Intra-Product, and Inter-Product Trade

Context and Issue

"Intra-industry trade" is commonly defined as an international exchange in which a given country both exports and imports the same good. This seems to be straightforward, but complications arise right away.[1]

The phrase "the same good" is obviously the major element of the definition. But what is actually meant by this phrase is crucially an outcome of classification. This is true not just when concrete estimations are involved, but also in attempting to understand the meaning of the term.

Suppose "wool" and "yarn" were classified under the same category, and thus would be regarded as "the same good". In this case, a major element of British trade over generations would appear as "intra-industry trade". While this would be true, given the classification, it would obviously be counterintuitive to most observers of trade patterns. Indeed, no such scheme

---

[1] In their path-breaking study, Grubel and Lloyd (1975) define the term as follows: "[The term "intra-industry trade"] describes aptly the international trade in differentiated products because commonly used statistical trade classification schemes result in much of this trade as showing up as the simultaneous export and import of products belonging to the same industry", (p. 1). Trade in differentiated products appears here not as explaining intra-industry trade but as defining it. This, we believe, is too restrictive. In particular, it does not allow for the distinction, to be elaborated shortly, between intra-product and inter-product trade.

of classification has traditionally been used. On the other hand, many less glaring cases do exist, in which products that belong to various grades of processing — sometimes one used as an input in producing the other (as in "wool" and "yarn") — are in fact classified together as a single "good", and a country's trade in these products will be regarded as "intra-industry" trade.

Thus, the definition at hand is inevitably a slave of the manner of classification. The designation of concrete transactions as "intra-industry" depends on the available schemes of classification, and on how we choose to employ these schemes.

"Similar" goods <u>cannot</u> be <u>identical</u>: an exchange of identical goods, when some transaction costs (of one form or another) must be involved, would normally not make sense. That is, the presumed "similar" goods must be — to some extent, and in one sense or another — different from each other. Two classes of such differences may be distinguished and they give rise to two separate categories of "intra-industry" trade. On the surface, they appear to be similar, but analytically they are radically different from each other. The distinction between the two is by now well-known, but there may be a need to sharpen it.

The first element is the exchange of two basically similar <u>final</u> goods, which appear under the same classified item. These are destined for final use. They are "basically similar" in the sense that they provide, in essence, very similar services to their user. But, in the perception of this user, they are slightly different from each other. Obvious examples are different brands of television sets, electric appliances, cars, or processed foods. The differentiation may be due to advertising, historic consumption traditions, differences in labeling, or similar factors. Trade of this nature has been the center of discussion and analysis for the last several decades, an analysis which is often referred to as the "new trade theory". It is due to a combination of economies of scale, existence of monopolistic competition, and some variation in customers' tastes. This element we shall refer to here as "inter-product trade".

The other element has gained particular attention in recent years. It is the outcome of the process by which the production of a final good is located in one country but incorporates the purchase of inputs from another country. This may involve, of course, more than one "round": the production of any input may itself require another input, imported still from another country. When the same components (i.e., the final good and its input) are <u>classified under the same item</u> an intra-industry trade will be recorded. This would be true for both the producer of the final good, which is the importer of the input, and for the exporter of the input, which would often be an importer of the final good. Examples of industries producing final goods which are often mentioned in this context — based on popular observations — include the automotive industry, electronics, electrical appliances, and the garment industry (clothing and leather goods). The phenomenon would probably appear to be even more widespread if trade in services were recorded (such as in computer facilities). We shall refer to this element of intra-industry trade as <u>intra-product</u> trade.

The weight of intra-product trade, not just in sheer size but as a fraction of aggregate trade in goods, is generally assumed to have grown substantially in recent years; it is "assumed" because good measurements are still missing, for reasons that will be noted shortly. Several factors must have contributed to such expansion.

One is the general, and remarkable, decline of trade barriers in the last two generations. In general, such reduction should lead to <u>any</u> trade expansion, not just intra-product trade. But, as mentioned, the latter may involve more than one "round" of input-output relationship. That is, an input may be imported and processed (but not to a final good), and the product then serves as a further input in the process of producing the final good. Since a tariff is a tax imposed on the <u>gross</u> value of an imported good, not on value added, this would imply double taxation on imported inputs. The overall removal (or reduction) of the tax would then encourage the import of such inputs in particular.

Next, probably of even larger importance, the substantial reduction of <u>transport costs</u> (in the narrow sense, i.e., shipping) must be noted. In this case, the relevant change is the <u>relative</u> reduction of costs which particularly applies to the traded inputs. The most important element must be the radical fall of costs of transportation <u>by air</u>, which has led to an expansion of this trade from almost nil two generations ago to a significant fraction of aggregate trade today. The traded inputs at hand are subject in particular to the impact of this factor. These are, in general, components (say, tubes rather than complete TV sets), with a high ratio of value to weight, which makes transportation by air relatively less expensive. Moreover, shipping by air facilitates an internationally-integrated production process by making the import of components fast and reliable, without the need to hold large inventories, thus making the availability of inputs produced locally less crucial.

A still further development, involving "costs" in a more general sense, is the drastic easing of communications. With communication in the modern age of computers allowing for instant connections of all forms almost anywhere on the globe, a system of command and control in a given center over faraway locations of production became highly developed and almost costless. This is an essential ingredient in a production process involving the diversification of loci of production of separate elements in the process.

Another development originating largely in a different area from the process of production is the dramatic reduction, in recent generations, of international barriers on the movement of <u>capital</u>. This has led, <u>inter-alia</u>, to a large expansion of foreign direct investment which in turn has encouraged the establishment and operation of multilateral firms. While the existence of this organizational form is not a necessary condition for an international geographical diversification of a production process, it undoubtedly facilitates and encourages such diversification, leading in this way to the expansion of intra-product trade.

We come back now to the distinction between inter- and intra-product trade. Although both appear as "intra-industry" trade, they originate from radically different sources. As noted, inter-product trade involves trade flows characterized by the "new trade theory", trade in similar final goods which are slightly differentiated and involve monopolistic competition, economies of scale, and variation of users' tastes.[2] Intra-product trade, on the other hand, involves flows of <u>different</u> products, at least one of which is an input into the other. Specialization and trade of this form originate from <u>differences in factor prices</u> (presumably most often due to differences in factors availabilities) among different geographic locations. This is, thus, trade which follows the classical Heckscher-Ohlin world. Intra- and inter-product trade thus belongs to the two "competing" (but complementing) basic models of the origin of international trade.

---

[2] Consult Linder (1961); Lancaster (1979); and Helpman and Krugman (1985).

We now move to the empirical analysis of intra-industry trade: its extent, its attributes, and their movement over time.

The basic indicator of the extent of intra-industry trade, which will be used throughout the study, is the following measure.[3]

$$IN_j = 1 - \frac{\sum_i \left| \frac{X_{ij}}{X_{.j}} - \frac{M_{ij}}{M_{.j}} \right|}{2},$$

where

IN_j = Index of Intra-industry trade for country j
X_{ij} = Exports of good i by country j
M_{ij} = Imports of good i by country j
$X_{.j}$ = Aggregate exports of country j, and
$M_{.j}$ = Aggregate imports of country j

Coverage, Period, and Method

The focus of our investigation will be the present characteristics. For convenience — certainly with no loss of relevance — we chose 2010 as representing the "present", rather than trying to advance it by a year or two even where sufficient data are available. While most of our analysis will address attributes at this point of time, we have also investigated changes over a long duration — essentially, the post-WWII period. We consider the year 1965 as the start of the period; prior to that year, data are sporadic, so that observations for such earlier years must be restricted to a partial selection of the world's countries — naturally, the more economically advanced countries (in fact, many present-day political entities had not even been independent countries in the decade or two immediately after WWII).

In principle, we include in our observation all present-day countries. The constraint on such inclusion is, naturally, availability of data. This is not a material restriction for present-day records: countries excluded on

---

[3]This formulation follows, with appropriate adaptations, the index of multilateral trade developed in Michaely (1962). Grubel and Lloyd (1975), after discussing this index along with others, use a slightly different variation of this index. One advantage of our formulation is that the use of shares in trade, rather than absolute sizes, serves to overcome the potential difficulty of a non-balanced country's trade.

this basis from 2010 observations constitute only an insignificant minority of the world's aggregate. But the further we dive into the past, the more countries are left out due to insufficient data (or, often, even due to their absence on the world map as independent entities). Thus, the longer is our period of search for changes over time, the more restrictive is the number of countries; but most of the world would still be covered.[4]

Change Over Time

We start with the analysis of long-term trends. Annex Table A.1 presents the intra-industry index for the years 1965 through 2010 in 5-year intervals. To make time-comparisons meaningful, it must refer to the same universe of countries at all points of time; hence, this analysis covers only countries for which data were available throughout the period 1965–2010. It includes, in fact, countries whose aggregate trade has formed, all throughout, an overwhelming share of total world trade. But it should be noted that this list is shorter than the more inclusive one which will be used further along when attributes of the <u>present</u> system are explored.

The intra-industry ratio has been estimated for each individual country and for each year of the period 1962–2010. But fully presenting this record would be highly space-consuming; hence it will be dispensed with here. Even presenting data in a more concise manner is avoided here, in the main text, and is relegated to Annex Table A.1. In this table, the estimated ratios are recorded in 5-year intervals, from 1965 to 2010. The presentation is limited to those countries, 53 in all, for which data are available throughout the period.

An overwhelming inference from this record stands out: the intensity of intra-industry trade increased almost universally, and in an impressive way. Of the 53 countries, the ratio at hand fell in only four of them, and most of the increases of the ratio in the large majority of countries — the other forty-nine — were remarkable.

Table 5.1 summarizes the record presented for the 53 countries in Table A.1. Several inferences are suggested by this table.

---

[4] Sources of data upon which the study is based may be obtained on request.

Table 5.1: Intra-industry ratios, averages, 1965–2010

	1965	1970	1975	1980	1985	1990	1995	2000	2005	2010
Mean	0.180	0.187	0.203	0.201	0.201	0.226	0.243	0.229	0.249	0.260
Median	0.113	0.156	0.165	0.152	0.157	0.176	0.209	0.168	0.201	0.227
Note	5.7	7.6	13.9	14.6	16.7	10.9	8.0	13.0	10.3	14.7

where 'Note' refers to percentage of oil in world exports.

First, a general upward trend of the intra-industry index appears to hold over the period as a whole, though not necessarily at a steady pace. Without being able to assign economic content to the numerical change, we note that the <u>mean</u> index increased, from 1965 to 2010, by close to 50 percent; while the <u>median</u> index even doubled.

Second, it appears that most of this increase took place up to 1995, whereas the change from then to 2010 — the last 15 years — was quite modest. By way of sheer speculation, this may raise the following inference. The factors leading to increased <u>intra</u>-product trade seem, from casual observations, to have been of particular relevance in the more recent period. Hence, the more impressive increase of intra-industry trade during earlier years probably reflects an increase of <u>inter</u>-product trade. The almost stagnation of intra-industry trade in more recent years must, in turn, when <u>intra</u>-product trade presumably prospered, reflect a <u>fall</u> of <u>inter</u>-product trade. This reasoning is only suggestive and speculative. To the extent that it does reflect reality, it indicates that <u>inter</u>-product trade tended to increase in the earlier post-war period but, to the contrary, to <u>fall</u> in more recent years.[5]

We also note that the increase of intra-industry trade was substantial up to 1975, but does <u>not</u> appear for the sub-period between 1975 and 1985. Offhand we cannot suggest an easy interpretation to these tendencies; this would require a more elaborate investigation of the structure of trade.[6]

---

[5] In his Nobel Lecture (2009), P. Krugman also made a suggestion indicating such shifting trends. It may be summarized in the statement that, "Both new geography and new trade, then, may describe forces that are waning rather than gathering strength."

[6] In part, this may probably be explained by changes in the level (proportion) of trade in oil — recorded as a Note in Table 1 — which primarily reflect fluctuations in oil prices.

Attributes and Determinants of Intra-Industry Trade

Table 5.2 provides the basic set of indices, or data, on which most of the following analysis will draw. It lists five such measures. They will be introduced and discussed in turn as the analysis progresses. Column (1) presents the basic index on which this analysis focuses, namely, the ratio of intra-industry trade.

One inference immediately comes to mind: A large degree of variance exists among the indices for individual countries: they range from as low as 0.004 (for the Maldives and Myanmar) to as high as 0.736 (for Singapore).[7] For the universe of countries studied, the mean is 0.250 and the median 0.211. The share of world exports involved in intra-industry trade (which amounts, in essence, to an export-weighted mean of the individual countries' indices) — not shown in the table — amounts in 2010 to 47.4 percent; that is practically to a half.

However, it also appears immediately that the levels of the index do not vary sporadically all around but tend to congregate in <u>regional</u> groups. In particular, a glaring difference appears when comparing Sub-Saharan Africa with Europe. In 27 Sub-Saharan African countries,[8] the median level of the intra-trade index is 0.145, about half the median level of the index for the aggregate of countries. For 32 European countries,[9] in con-

---

In 1975, 1980, and 1985, with the remarkable increase in oil prices, the proportion of oil exports in aggregate world exports increased from an earlier level of 6–7 percent to roughly a level of 15 percent. Except in instances of mostly transit trade, as remarkably in Singapore's trade, oil is not a product subject to intra-industry trade, and it is universally of much importance. An increased share of oil in world trade would thus tend to lower the overall share of intra-industry trade.

[7] Since Singapore's trade constitutes to a large extent of transit trade, this high index may not represent "normal" trade. The next highest index is pretty close, though: 0.724 for Belgium.

[8] These are: Benin, Botswana, Burkina Faso, Burundi, Central Af. Rep., Congo, Cote d'Ivoire, Ethiopia, Gambia, Ghana, Kenya, Lesotho, Malawi, Mali, Mauritania, Mauritius, Mozambique, Namibia, Niger, Nigeria, Rwanda, Senegal, South Africa, Togo, Uganda, Zambia and Zimbabwe.

[9] These cover all European countries (including the islands — Malta, Cyprus, the UK, Ireland and Iceland), save the republics of the former Soviet Union.

Table 5.2: Basic indices and data, 2010

Country	Intra-Industry Ratio (1)	Per-Capita GDP (2)	Aggregate GDP (3)	Coefficient of Diversification (4)	Similarity Index (5)
Afghanistan	0.029	569.9	15936.8	0.723	0.415
Albania	0.251	4094.4	11927.0	0.855	0.331
Algeria	0.012	4473.5	161207.3	0.655	0.030
Andorra	0.331	39639.4	3346.3	0.851	0.399
Antigua and Barbuda	0.283	13017.3	1135.5	0.731	0.287
Argentina	0.262	11198.6	425916.1	0.888	0.329
Armenia	0.169	3124.8	9260.3	0.800	0.226
Aruba	0.384	24289.1	2467.7	0.608	0.292
Australia	0.324	51845.7	1142250.5	0.858	0.292
Austria	0.631	46659.8	390235.1	0.930	0.734
Azerbaijan	0.041	5842.8	52902.7	0.613	0.070
Bahamas	0.069	21920.5	7909.6	0.782	0.353
Bahrain	0.145	20386.0	25713.3	0.621	0.207
Bangladesh	0.050	760.3	115279.1	0.759	0.136
Barbados	0.323	15901.4	4445.5	0.842	0.426
Belarus	0.257	5818.9	55220.9	0.856	0.410
Belgium	0.752	44382.9	483577.5	0.913	0.828
Belize	0.030	4344.1	1397.1	0.769	0.035
Benin	0.243	733.0	6970.2	0.702	0.438
Bhutan	0.092	2201.3	1585.5	0.786	0.191
Bolivia (Plurinational St)	0.065	1981.2	19649.6	0.798	0.076
Bosnia Herzegovina	0.309	4475.1	17163.1	0.894	0.448
Botswana	0.148	6244.0	12786.7	0.550	0.248
Brazil	0.334	11121.4	2208872.2	0.898	0.380
Bulgaria	0.369	6752.6	49939.2	0.906	0.547
Burkina Faso	0.118	574.5	8980.0	0.589	0.055
Burundi	0.032	214.2	2026.9	0.639	0.070
Cabo Verde	0.068	3393.9	1664.3	0.720	0.039

(*Continued*)

Table 5.2:   (*Continued*)

Country	Intra-Industry Ratio (1)	Per-Capita GDP (2)	Aggregate GDP (3)	Coefficient of Diversification (4)	Similarity Index (5)
Cambodia	0.042	782.7	11242.3	0.737	0.093
Cameroon	0.243	1147.2	23622.5	0.767	0.307
Canada	0.572	47445.8	1613406.1	0.906	0.608
Central African Rep.	0.216	446.8	1986.0	0.678	0.039
Chile	0.112	12785.1	217538.3	0.759	0.169
China	0.370	4514.9	6039658.5	0.917	0.425
China, Hong Kong SAR	0.844	32550.0	228637.7	0.890	0.879
China, Macao SAR	0.363	52604.3	28123.6	0.704	0.206
Colombia	0.210	6250.7	287018.2	0.843	0.263
Comoros	0.019	739.9	517.0	0.534	0.035
Congo	0.499	2953.2	20523.3	0.601	0.350
Cook Isds	0.012			0.605	0.505
Costa Rica	0.349	7986.0	36298.3	0.885	0.450
Croatia	0.400	13509.2	59680.6	0.915	0.564
Cuba	0.088	5688.7	64328.2	0.790	10.000
Cyprus	0.327	30438.9	25247.4	0.867	0.450
Czech Rep.	0.615	19764.0	207015.9	0.922	0.719
Cote d'Ivoire	0.380	1236.1	24884.5	0.768	0.254
Denmark	0.597	57647.7	319811.0	0.919	0.679
Dominica	0.087	6937.3	493.7	0.757	0.159
Dominican Rep.	0.187	5442.0	53864.5	0.875	0.312
Ecuador	0.124	4657.3	69555.4	0.714	0.182
Egypt	0.191	2668.0	218888.3	0.863	0.416
El Salvador	0.296	3547.1	21418.3	0.858	0.405
Estonia	0.497	14641.4	19494.7	0.905	0.713
Ethiopia	0.059	341.9	29933.8	0.760	0.081
FS Micronesia	0.013	2838.4	294.1	0.439	1.000
Faeroe Isds	0.154	47381.5	2301.2	0.626	1.000

Table 5.2: *(Continued)*

Country	Intra-Industry Ratio (1)	Per-Capita GDP (2)	Aggregate GDP (3)	Coefficient of Diversification (4)	Similarity Index (5)
Fiji	0.178	3652.0	3140.5	0.824	0.438
Finland	0.405	46205.2	247814.6	0.880	0.523
Fmr Sudan	0.100			0.544	0.019
France	0.678	40705.8	2646994.7	0.927	0.733
French Polynesia	0.094			0.644	0.121
Gabon	0.029	9312.0	14358.6	0.508	1.000
Gambia	0.152	562.6	952.4	0.756	0.238
Georgia	0.150	2964.5	11638.5	0.849	0.254
Germany	0.688	41788.0	3417298.0	0.919	0.763
Ghana	0.051	1323.1	32174.8	0.685	0.095
Greece	0.400	26919.4	299379.4	0.899	0.511
Greenland	0.034	40193.7	2287.2	0.729	0.102
Grenada	0.114	7365.7	771.0	0.767	1.000
Guatemala	0.272	2806.0	41338.0	0.891	0.364
Guinea	0.025	430.1	4736.0	0.686	1.000
Guinea-Bissau	0.001	518.6	847.5	0.414	1.000
Guyana	0.057	2998.9	2259.3	0.762	0.065
Honduras	0.168	2110.8	15839.3	0.820	0.247
Hungary	0.544	13009.3	130093.8	0.903	0.728
Iceland	0.112	41620.1	13236.9	0.744	0.148
India	0.303	1387.9	1708458.9	0.892	0.434
Indonesia	0.268	3125.2	755094.2	0.905	0.376
Iran	0.089	6299.9	467790.2	0.627	0.218
Ireland	0.363	48260.7	220076.1	0.854	0.466
Israel	0.423	30736.4	234321.7	0.778	0.535
Italy	0.553	35851.5	2125184.8	0.937	0.615
Jamaica	0.140	4902.0	13190.5	0.782	0.357
Japan	0.378	42935.3	5498717.8	0.904	0.401

(Continued)

Table 5.2: *(Continued)*

Country	Intra-Industry Ratio (1)	Per-Capita GDP (2)	Aggregate GDP (3)	Coefficient of Diversification (4)	Similarity Index (5)
Jordan	0.310	4054.3	26425.4	0.888	0.414
Kazakhstan	0.075	9070.6	148047.3	0.685	0.130
Kenya	0.182	991.9	39999.7	0.846	0.289
Kiribati	0.010	1465.5	150.4	0.745	0.055
Kyrgyzstan	0.153	880.0	4794.4	0.797	0.224
Latvia	0.479	11319.5	23743.3	0.920	0.650
Lebanon	0.384	8763.8	38010.0	0.898	0.400
Lesotho	0.129	1088.0	2187.5	0.807	0.216
Libya	0.008	11933.8	74773.4	0.497	0.023
Lithuania	0.460	11988.8	37132.6	0.881	0.540
Luxembourg	0.370	103267.3	52351.7	0.903	0.503
Madagascar	0.138	414.1	8729.9	0.870	0.249
Malawi	0.111	471.2	6959.7	0.680	0.130
Malaysia	0.499	9069.0	255016.9	0.887	0.657
Maldives	0.034	6330.8	2323.4	0.659	0.009
Mali	0.059	704.1	10678.7	0.595	0.083
Malta	0.249	19694.1	8163.4	0.793	0.546
Mauritania	0.001	1207.8	4337.8	0.637	0.010
Mauritius	0.265	7772.1	9718.2	0.836	0.306
Mayotte	0.253			0.857	1.000
Mexico	0.491	8861.5	1051128.6	0.900	0.579
Mongolia	0.030	2650.3	7189.5	0.734	1.000
Montenegro	0.196	6682.3	4139.2	0.769	0.271
Montserrat	0.092			0.693	0.500
Morocco	0.143	2857.7	93216.7	0.882	0.259
Mozambique	0.073	417.5	10154.2	0.643	0.159
Myanmar	0.005			0.769	0.011
Namibia	0.200	5143.1	11282.2	0.815	0.257

Table 5.2: (*Continued*)

Country	Intra-Industry Ratio (1)	Per-Capita GDP (2)	Aggregate GDP (3)	Coefficient of Diversification (4)	Similarity Index (5)
Nepal	0.091	595.4	16002.7	0.894	0.204
Neth. Antilles	0.319			0.870	1.000
Netherlands	0.711	50341.3	836439.7	0.887	0.804
New Caledonia	0.026			0.602	0.041
New Zealand	0.293	33692.2	146584.5	0.877	0.321
Nicaragua	0.115	1523.5	8741.3	0.829	0.128
Niger	0.285	351.0	5718.6	0.729	0.174
Nigeria	0.034	2315.0	369062.5	0.637	0.061
Norway	0.296	87646.3	428524.7	0.767	0.305
Oman	0.129	19920.6	58641.4	0.641	0.200
Pakistan	0.084	1043.3	177406.9	0.858	0.218
Panama	0.396	7987.1	28917.2	0.814	0.720
Paraguay	0.073	3225.6	20030.5	0.782	0.076
Peru	0.090	5056.3	148521.8	0.833	0.193
Philippines	0.291	2145.2	199590.8	0.777	0.407
Poland	0.528	12597.5	479242.5	0.926	0.656
Portugal	0.468	22540.0	238317.6	0.927	0.612
Qatar	0.023	70870.2	125122.3	0.647	0.030
Rep. of Korea	0.410		1094499.3	0.895	0.514
Rep. of Moldova	0.232	22151.2	5811.6	0.842	0.347
Romania	0.384	8297.5	167998.1	0.914	0.598
Russian Federation	0.158	10675.0	1524917.5	0.801	0.224
Rwanda	0.121	553.6	5698.5	0.744	0.150
Saint Kitts and Nevis	0.118	13227.0	692.5	0.737	0.229
Saint Lucia	0.328	7043.5	1249.5	0.803	1.000
Saint Vincent and the Grenadines	0.159		681.2	0.819	0.208
Samoa	0.039	3530.6	656.8	0.671	0.193

(*Continued*)

Table 5.2: (*Continued*)

Country	Intra-Industry Ratio (1)	Per-Capita GDP (2)	Aggregate GDP (3)	Coefficient of Diversification (4)	Similarity Index (5)
Sao Tome and Principe	0.084	1142.2	195.2	0.476	0.057
Saudi Arabia	0.108	18754.0	526811.5	0.586	0.109
Senegal	0.242	998.1	12932.4	0.863	0.410
Serbia	0.366	5411.9	39460.4	0.922	0.501
Seychelles	0.106	10804.7	969.9	0.632	1.000
Singapore	0.714	46569.7	236421.8	0.852	0.786
Slovakia	0.514	16554.9	236421.8	0.905	0.655
Slovenia	0.537	23438.8	48016.4	0.912	0.673
Solomon Isds	0.017	1276.3	671.6	0.504	0.048
South Africa	0.279	7392.9	375349.4	0.889	0.407
Spain	0.609	30737.8	1431672.8	0.921	0.676
Sri Lanka	0.103	2819.7	56725.7	0.844	0.202
Suriname	0.219	8430.9	4368.4	0.522	0.114
Swaziland	0.252	2956.7	3527.8	0.749	1.000
Sweden	0.566	52076.4	488379.3	0.910	0.709
Switzerland	0.581	74277.1	581211.7	0.872	0.632
Syria	0.158			0.754	0.305
TFYR of Macedonia	0.210	4561.2	9407.2	0.885	0.345
Thailand	0.416	5111.9	340923.6	0.926	0.539
Timor-Leste	0.131	875.8	934.0	0.771	1.000
Togo	0.183	496.5	3172.9	0.814	0.278
Tonga	0.013	3557.7	369.8	0.708	0.044
Trinidad and Tobago	0.195	15840.4	21037.6	0.790	0.283
Tunisia	0.267	4176.6	44050.9	0.884	0.415
Turkey	0.336	10111.5	731168.1	0.926	0.479
Turks and Caicos Isds	0.145			0.733	1.000
Tuvalu	0.033	3238.4	31.8	0.635	1.000
USA	0.573	48374.1	14964372.0	0.924	0.638

Table 5.2: *(Continued)*

Country	Intra-Industry Ratio (1)	Per-Capita GDP (2)	Aggregate GDP (3)	Coefficient of Diversification (4)	Similarity Index (5)
Uganda	0.228	608.8	20181.8	0.848	0.356
Ukraine	0.259	2974.0	136419.3	0.880	0.385
United Arab Emirates	0.637	34341.9	286049.3	0.705	0.614
UK	0.638	38292.9	2403504.3	0.912	0.766
United Rep. of Tanzania	0.103	708.5	31407.9	0.841	0.202
Uruguay	0.170	11938.3	40284.7	0.848	0.258
Vanuatu	0.081	2965.8	700.8	0.813	0.170
Venezuela	0.068	13581.4	393801.5	0.609	0.049
Viet Nam	0.187	1333.6	115931.7	0.882	0.344
Yemen	0.091	1310.1	30906.8	0.564	0.152
Zambia	0.099	1456.1	20265.6	0.630	0.171
Zimbabwe	0.086	674.3	9422.2	0.842	0.138

trast, the median level of the index is as high as 0.541, twice the median level for the aggregate countries, and about four times the median level for Sub-Saharan Africa. Put differently, among Sub-Saharan African countries, in only five out of the population of 27 countries does the level of the index exceed, and even then, only slightly, the median level of the index for the universe of countries. Among European countries, on the other hand, only in one country, Iceland, out of 32 does the level of the intra-industry index fall below this median. The contrast between these two groups of countries is glaring. In a more general way, it may be said that a high level of intra-industry trade characterizes the trade of Europe.

But Europe is obviously not alone. It is a continent (or most of it) of countries with specific characterization. They are historically trade partners, relatively close to each other, which tend to share several important attributes. These observations are important, but are not of much relevance to the specific phenomenon under investigation. What does seem relevant, on the other hand, is the fact that most, if not all, European countries are highly economically advanced. Indeed, a cursory look at Table 5.2 should immediately suggest that advanced, high-income economies tend to exhibit a relatively high level of intra-industry trade. We test this proposition by means of relating the data of column (1) in Table 5.2 with those presented in column (2), which provide the per-capita income level of each of the countries under investigation. The relationship of the two is tested by two alternative coefficients. One is the "conventional" coefficient (Pearson), yielded by regressing the intra-industry index (column (1)) on the per-capita income level (Column (2)). The other is the Spearman rank correlation coefficient which may probably give a better illustration when no quantitative relationship is sought. The two correlation coefficients are, in turn, 0.541 (Pearson) and 0.575 (Spearman). Both coefficients happen to be almost identical and are significant at practically any desired level. These, we suggest, are high enough to indicate a clear association of the strength of a country's intra-industry trade with its level of (per-capita) income. Given our earlier discussion of the sources of intra-industry trade, this inference is, of course, not surprising.

Yet another important attribute of an economy which may be related to the intensity of intra-industry trade is the size of the economy, best represented by the level of its aggregate income.[10] The reason for such a potential relationship is similar to the one discussed right now in reference to the impact of per-capita income level; the larger the economy, the more diversified its structure is expected to be. The level of aggregate income is presented in column (3) of Table 5.2. As with the level of per-capita income, the relationship of this attribute to the intensity of intra-industry trade appears to be quite strong. The Pearson correlation coefficient of the two (columns (1) and (3)) is found to be 0.313, and the Spearman rank correlation coefficient is 0.562. Both these coefficients are significant at any desired level and may be judged to be pretty high, particularly the latter.

Both attributes — the levels of per-capita and of aggregate income — have been assumed, a-priori, to be relevant to the intensity of intra-industry trade due to their impact on the structure of the economy, including, most importantly for the analysis at hand, the structure of its trade.[11] We move

---

[10] Such a relationship is suggested, though not tested, in Grubel and Lloyd (op. cit.).

[11] This is most probably true not just for supply but also for the demand patterns of the economy; the higher the income level, the more diversified the demand structure, the more

now to observe directly the impact of this structure on intra-industry trade. For this purpose, we construct an index of <u>diversification</u> of trade. We restrict our observation to <u>exports</u> since measurements of the imports trade commonly tend to show only a small variance among nations. The degree of diversification is represented by the Gini-Hirschman coefficient. The measure is presented in Column (4) of Table 5.2.[12]

A regression analysis relating the level of intra-industry trade to that of the degree of commodity diversification of the country's exports yields a (Pearson) correlation coefficient of 0.640; the (Spearman) rank correlation coefficient is found to be 0.751. Both coefficients, again, significant of any practically desired level, appear to be high indeed, even substantially higher than those representing the relationship between intra-industry ratios and the levels of GDP per capita, and aggregate GDP.

But these three separate investigations of the relationship of the intra-industry index to, respectively, the level of per-capita income, of aggregate income, and the degree of commodity diversification suffer from an obvious flaw. Clearly, these three "explanatory" variables must be correlated with each other; the relationship of <u>per-capita</u> and of <u>aggregate</u> income levels needs no explanation, and the presumed impact of both of these on the commodity structure of exports has just been emphasized in our analysis.[13] Hence, a multiple-regression analysis is in order; it yields the findings recorded in Table 5.3.

---

likely the existence of intra-industry trade — particularly of its inter-product component. We see, however, no clear-cut channel of empirically pursuing this proposition.

[12] The Gini-Hirschman coefficient of commodity concentration (See Michaely, 1962) is defined as:

$$C_{jx} = \sqrt{\sum_i \left(\frac{x_{ij}}{x_{\cdot j}}\right)^2}$$

where

X_{ij} = export of commodity i by country j; and
$X_{\cdot j}$ = aggregate export of country j

Note that this is a coefficient of <u>concentration</u>. To adjust it to our needs, we turn it into its obverse, a coefficient of <u>diversification</u>:

$$D_{jk} = 1 - C_{jx}$$

[13] More rigorously, the association of these three variables with each other is as follows: For per-capita income and aggregate income, the Pearson correlation coefficient is 0.266,

Table 5.3: Correlation coefficients of the intra-industry ratio with

	Per-Capita GDP (1)	Aggregate GDP (2)	Coefficient of Diversification (3)
Pearson Correlation	0.541	0.313	0.640
Spearman (rank) Correlation	0.575	0.562	0.751

All these coefficients are significant at any desired level. And they all seem to indicate a strong association of the intra-industry intensity with the attributes at hand. The strongest association, it appears, is with the level of commodity diversification. This, given the reasoning advanced earlier, should not be surprising.

Given the nature and the presumed origins of intra-industry trade — both inter- and intra-product — its relationship to the nature of trade should be expected to be more intensive when <u>manufactured</u> products are concerned rather than when mostly raw-material based products are involved. To test this hypothesis, we estimated the intra-industry ratios separately for the group of commodities whose classification indicates the predominance of manufacturing activity.[14] That is, the aggregate of these groups is taken as the universe of trade transactions. The expectation is indeed borne out. For 164 countries, the mean ratio of intra-industry trade is found to be 0.353, in comparison with the mean of 0.250 found earlier for the entire universe of countries. Moreover, if the individual country ratios are <u>weighted</u> by the size of exports of each country, the weighted mean increases to as high as 0.525, considerably higher than the mean ratio of European countries. Thus, on average, roughly a half of aggregate trade in manufactures shares the attribute of intra-industry trade.

Finally, in Column (5) of Table 5.2, we present an index which expresses the degree of <u>similarity</u> of the commodity composition of a

---

and the Spearman rank correlation coefficient is 0.505. For the coefficient of diversification and the level of per-capita income the correlation coefficients are, respectively, 0.251 and 0.371. And, finally, for aggregate income and diversification, 0.244 and 0.579.

[14]These are the products included in the broad categories 6, 7 and 8 of the SITC.

country's export and import flows (once more, at the SITC 3-digit level).[15] It seems obvious that the strength of intra-industry trade should be closely related to this export-import relationship. To cite the two extremes: if <u>none</u> of the goods exported are also imported — a similarity index of zero — no intra-industry trade at all would be found. At the other extreme, if <u>all</u> goods are represented equally in the export and import flows (in absolute values or, as defined here, in shares of the aggregates), <u>all</u> trade transactions would assume the intra-industry character.

As before, we regress the index of intra-industry on that of the export-import similarity. The yielded Pearson coefficient of correlation of the two is 0.909; and the Spearman rank correlation coefficient is 0.887. Both coefficients are similar; not surprisingly, they are very high. Indeed, they are close enough to unity as for the two indices to be regarded as perfectly correlated with each other. Thus, the coefficient of export-import similarity of commodity structures may serve as a perfect proxy of the level of a country's intensity of intra-industry trade.

Upon reflection, it should be clear why these two indices are so closely related; they reflect the same phenomenon, in different ways. The intra-industry index refers to the export-import relationship in any trade flows of a given good by contrasting exports and imports <u>directly</u>; whereas the similarity index does it by contrasting <u>shares</u> in aggregate trade. Thus, the similarity index does not "explain" the level of intra-industry trade; rather, it may serve as an alternative measure of evaluating the intensity of this phenomenon.

---

[15] $S_j = 1 - \Sigma \left| \frac{X_{ij}}{X_{.j}} - \frac{M_{ij}}{M_{.j}} \right|$ where, as before:

$X_{.j}$, M_{ij} = exports and imports of good i by country j
$X_{.j}$, M_{ij} = aggregate exports and imports of country j; and
| | stands for absolute values.
The index ranges from zero to unity.
The index is provided in Michaely (1962).

Annex Table 5.4: Intra-industry ratios, 1965–2010

	1965	1970	1975	1980	1985	1990	1995	2000	2005	2010	Ratio, 2010/1965
Argentina	0.068	0.252	0.224	0.152	0.192	0.257	0.327	0.352	0.345	0.303	4.45
Australia	0.193	0.344	0.342	0.220			0.236	0.222	0.154	0.122	0.63
Austria	0.408	0.458	0.483	0.480	0.320	0.368	0.259	0.273	0.341	0.305	0.76
Belgium–Lux	0.442	0.478	0.518	0.671	0.591	0.602	0.661	0.716	0.752	0.752	1.70
Bolivia	0.001	0.001	0.001	0.001	0.006	0.085	0.075	0.125	0.084	0.045	45.00
Brazil	0.112	0.189	0.257	0.183	0.158	0.219	0.299	0.315	0.341	0.327	2.92
Cameroon	0.140	0.142	0.137	0.014		0.076	0.046	0.180	0.205	0.281	2.01
Canada	0.293	0.295	0.386	0.191	0.196	0.491	0.515	0.571	0.600	0.543	1.85
Chile	0.010	0.016	0.027	0.031	0.028	0.045	0.085	0.091	0.126	0.097	9.70
Colombia	0.043	0.084	0.218	0.063	0.054	0.068	0.176	0.213	0.228	0.192	4.47
Costa Rica	0.047	0.340	0.286	0.298	0.254	0.143	0.193	0.282	0.354	0.344	7.32
Denmark	0.427	0.475	0.471	0.442	0.442	0.487	0.504	0.587	0.582	0.611	1.43
Ecuador	0.125	0.082	0.001	0.019	0.198	0.017	0.085	0.113	0.117	0.131	1.05
Egypt	0.171	0.090	0.147	0.017	0.037	0.078	0.119	0.121	0.168	0.214	1.25
El Salvador	0.260	0.282	0.235	0.306	0.237	0.331	0.226	0.296	0.301	0.287	1.10
Finland	0.163	0.235	0.262	0.280	0.296	0.351	0.349	0.378	0.424	0.386	1.88
France	0.546	0.591	0.545	0.610	0.604	0.624	0.683	0.693	0.688	0.668	1.22
Germany Fed. Rep.	0.472	0.540	0.504	0.587	0.600	0.637	0.631	0.662	0.689	0.687	1.46

Greece	0.097	0.102	0.111	0.127	0.180	0.234	0.304	0.371	0.406	0.394	4.06
Guatemala	0.058	0.290	0.294	0.293	0.269	0.213	0.209	0.252	0.271	0.273	4.71
Honduras	0.034	0.156	0.132	0.139	0.075	0.070	0.069	0.113	0.178	0.158	4.65
Hong Kong, China SAR	0.385	0.303	0.406	0.133	0.587	0.698	0.782	0.815	0.838	0.850	2.21
Iceland	0.065	0.068	0.065	0.001	0.023	0.061	0.089	0.113	0.104	0.119	1.83
Ireland	0.155	0.176	0.429	0.375	0.366	0.421	0.442	0.461	0.357	0.369	2.38
Israel	0.114	0.127	0.217	0.206	0.188	0.254	0.332	0.371	0.435	0.411	3.61
Italy	0.353	0.382	0.370	0.408	0.419	0.459	0.489	0.523	0.547	0.560	1.59
Japan	0.157	0.209	0.144	0.206	0.208	0.277	0.323	0.389	0.397	0.360	2.29
Jordan	0.218	0.243	0.285	0.311	0.286	0.249	0.277	0.381	0.318	0.303	1.39
Korea, Rep. of	0.073	0.084	0.155	0.206	0.392	0.304	0.383	0.417	0.416	0.403	5.50
Madagascar	0.050	0.071	0.016	0.021	0.033	0.046	0.034	0.164	0.119	0.157	3.14
Malaysia	0.398	0.226	0.339	0.192	0.226	0.300	0.375	0.436	0.504	0.494	1.24
Malta	0.140	0.166	0.178	0.169	0.191	0.121	0.308	0.445	0.245	0.254	1.81
Mexico	0.101	0.182	0.189	0.072	0.155	0.295	0.466	0.496	0.497	0.485	4.80
Morocco	0.049	0.054	0.061	0.025	0.043	0.064	0.086	0.118	0.143	0.143	2.92
Netherlands	0.502	0.560	0.522	0.555	0.580	0.604	0.663	0.694	0.711	0.712	1.42
New Zealand	0.055	0.121	0.147	0.188	0.179	0.233	0.266	0.281	0.313	0.273	4.96
Nicaragua	0.027	0.214	0.245	0.166	0.101	0.134	0.066	0.096	0.146	0.084	3.11
Peru	0.016	0.020	0.064	0.055	0.038	0.044	0.065	0.092	0.086	0.093	5.81
Philippines	0.008	0.019	0.056	0.072	0.195	0.267	0.335	0.389	0.455	0.482	60.25

(Continued)

Annex Table 5.4: *(Continued)*

	1965	1970	1975	1980	1985	1990	1995	2000	2005	2010	Ratio, 2010/1965
Portugal	0.122	0.156	0.155	0.152	0.194	0.267	0.335	0.389	0.454	0.482	3.95
Senegal	0.124	0.287	0.241	0.181		0.131	0.130	0.146	0.252	0.232	1.87
Singapore	0.640	0.515	0.472	0.520	0.542	0.624	0.734	0.737	0.464	0.562	0.88
Spain	0.148	0.287	0.290	0.333	0.342	0.495	0.566	0.598	0.615	0.604	4.08
Sri Lanka	0.024	0.015	0.021	0.028	0.065	0.075		0.124	0.110	0.096	4.00
Sweden	0.381	0.406	0.428	0.389	0.409	0.482	0.531	0.540	0.559	0.572	1.50
Switzerland	0.412	0.437	0.458	0.503	0.496	0.537	0.541	0.591	0.596	0.566	1.37
Thailand	0.067	0.079	0.082	0.064	0.109	0.222	0.294	0.374	0.400	0.433	6.45
Togo	0.212	0.292	0.272	0.182		0.074	0.230	0.130	0.162	0.204	0.96
Tunisia	0.069	0.065	0.111	0.140	0.129	0.199	0.210	0.224	0.256	0.279	4.04
Turkey	0.005	0.013	0.029	0.029	0.200	0.179	0.212	0.273	0.306	0.367	73.40
UK	0.374	0.465	0.482	0.613	0.588	0.611	0.676	0.675	0.652	0.625	1.67
USA	0.258	0.328	0.266	0.376	0.390	0.548	0.580	0.589	0.569	0.576	2.23
Venezuela	0.005	0.008	0.012	0.026	0.032	0.141	0.151	0.104	0.081	0.055	11.00

Chapter 6

The Impact of Distance:
A Non-Newtonian Analysis

The Issue[1]

The impact of distance on the size of trade among potential partners has been an important subject of the research of international trade flows in the last few decades. Appreciation of this impact is an essential component for issues such as the determination of promising partners for preferential trade agreements, or for the consideration of the need for the grant of compensating special privileges in international agreements for countries with inherent weaknesses in the conduct of international trade.[2]

Most often, the study of the impact of distance has been conducted within the framework of the "gravity model", or "gravity equation".[3] Borrowing from the Newtonian equation in physics, this model starts with the presumption that the size of a trade flow between two partners is a function of "distance", geographic distance between the two partners, and "mass", the size of each partner's income. Within this framework, the impact of distance is separated and estimated.

---

[1] This section draws partly on Michaely (2009).

[2] See for instance, for recent contributions, various studies in the volume of *WTO at the Margins* (2006).

[3] For some salient contributions to the development of this model, see Tinbergen (1962), Linneman (1966), Anderson (1979), and Bergstrand (1985, 1990).

Almost invariably, these "gravity-model" studies have found a predominant influence of distance on the size of trade flows. The elasticity of the trade-distance relationship appears most often to be in the range of unity and above.[4] Thus, for instance, hypothetically doubling the distance between two potential partners would cut their mutual trade flows by half; tripling the distance would lower the trade flows to just one third. This is a dramatic impact indeed.[5] But these findings stand in obvious contradiction to estimates of the costs which must be involved in distance — transportation costs cannot possibly explain the presumed impact of distance on trade. Available studies of transportation costs come up with estimates in the range of 3–10% of the cost excluding international transfer costs. That is, the C.I.F to F.O.B price ratio is in the range of 1.03–1.10.[6]

Moreover, <u>marginal</u> costs of (international) transportation must be substantially below average costs, since much of the transportation costs components are of a fixed nature. This includes elements such as packing, loading and unloading of the cargo, waiting time in ports, or paper work such as consular registration, etc. Thus, for instance, doubling the distance a cargo has to travel should raise transportation costs by significantly less. But even putting aside this difference between marginal and average costs, the change in transportation costs due to a change in distance must be rather trivial. Take again a doubling of distance, and suppose that transportation costs are 10% of the F.O.B. price to start with, and that they double with the doubling of distance. The C.I.F. price would then increase by almost 10% — from 1.1 to 1.2 of the F.O.B. price. Expecting such price changes to lower the quantity demanded and transacted by half would require an incredibly high elasticity of demand by the customer country of levels which intuitively exceed any reasonable expectations.

---

[4] Disidier and Head (2008) summarizes the estimates of the relationship at hand in over 100 studies, which among them contain about 1,500 estimates. The trade distance elasticity appears almost universally to be within the range of –0.5 to –1.5, with the mean and the mode being close to unity.

[5] A recent study, Helpman, Melitz, and Rubinstein (2008), conducted along different lines from the conventional "gravity model", argues that the estimates inferred by this convention suffer from an upward bias. But even in this study, the estimated elasticity is around –0.6 to –0.7.

[6] See, for instance, Moneta (1959), Hummels (2001), or Redding and Venables (2006).

This contradiction has certainly not escaped attention. In a general way, reconciliation has been attempted by observing that distance may not just imply a price differential, due to transportation costs, but may stand for other elements which may affect the size of mutual trade. One is a shared border; proximate countries may have common borders, which presumably tend to increase trade flows among partners. Other elements work in a similar way. Proximate countries, more so than others, may be expected to share important cultural attributes (a common language is obviously the most important), or to share histories, religion, legal or political systems, all of which are elements conducive to trade. But, while true, it should be noticed that the estimates of trade-distance elasticity mentioned earlier do, mostly, take these non-price elements into account and try to separate them out, normally through the use of dummy variables. The aforementioned elasticities are thus derived after the impact of the non-price proximity elements has been abstracted from.

A more recent response to the apparent counter–intuitive estimates of the trade-distance elasticity is that "distance" stands primarily for "information costs". This concept, which presumably incorporates other elements than those of the (estimated) impact of shared borders, shared language, etc., is rather elusive and probably unquantifiable (except, as in the present argument, as an inference derived from residuals). To the extent that there is much substance to it, this might have been more relevant to earlier generations: at present, information salient to the conduct of transactions presumably flows freely and immediately over the globe. But even if this element were important, it would at most imply that proximate countries would better share information than others. It definitely would not imply that an "information barrier" somehow increases, with distance, beyond a certain threshold. That is, it would not yield a linear estimate of the impact of distance. Rather, it would call for a different method of estimation, perhaps through the classification of countries into categories of "proximate" neighbors and others. Some such distinction will indeed be attempted in the present study.

We thus reach the almost inevitable conclusion that the impact of distance on trade inferred through the "gravity equation" estimates must have been grossly over-estimated. Perhaps a different approach may better serve for this task. To this we now turn.

Coverage and Construction of Observations

Our aim is to observe, in principle, all bilateral flows in today's world trade; in practice we fall slightly short of it, but the discrepancy is insignificant. Our basis of observations are trade data detailed by SITC for 2008. These are drawn from the United Nations commodity trade statistics database (COMTRADE).

We include in the study as many countries as would seem to be of some benefit without involving excessive costs. Trade data are available for the overwhelming majority of present independent (at least in the recording sense) countries and territories. In 2008, these numbered 201. But including all of them would be cumbersome, costly, and unhelpful; over half of these units are very minor actors, the knowledge of which would add only little in the present context.[7] We have thus decided to cover in the study only countries whose trade amounts (individually) to at least one seventh of 1 percent of world trade according to aggregated trade data published by the World Trade Organization. This leads to the inclusion of 82 countries, whose combined trade amounted to 98.24 percent of the world's aggregate. From these, only countries for which detailed trade data are available at the COMTRADE database were included in the analysis. This leads to the inclusion of 70 countries, whose combined trade amounted to 92.24 percent of the world's aggregate. This surely enables the establishment of a solid foundation for an empirical analysis; the aggregate number of (potential) bilateral trade flows among these countries is as high as 4,761. The list of countries, with their volumes of trade, is presented in the Appendix.

The first basic set of observations we establish is the volumes of bilateral trade flows among countries. The second basic set is that of bilateral distances among all countries covered in the study. This is drawn from a file containing the great circle distance between capital cities (Gleditsch, Kristian. Capdist.csv. http://ksgleditsch.com/data-5.html).

As we proceed, several other sets of data will be required; but these will be presented when the analyses for which they are used is discussed further along in the study.[8]

---

[7]The (potential) number of bilateral trade flows among all countries would exceed 40,000.

[8]An export flow of one country to its partner is identical, by definition, to an import flow between the two in the opposite direction. Hence, with perfect data and using proper definitions the universe of observations of import flows would be a mirror image of the

We shall employ two alternative, though inevitably related, forms of analysis. These two will be used to either reinforce or cast doubt upon the inferences of each other. The next section will address one of these methods, which may be characterized as semi-impressionistic, whereas the other — more rigorous — will be discussed in the following section.

Distance and the Volume of Trade Flows

The method of analysis used in this section is rudimentary. Having two sets of variables, one of the volumes of bilateral trade flows and the other of distances, what is the relationship between the two?

A rough impression may be gained, first, from a scatter diagram of the two variables, presented in Chart 6.1. The indication suggested by this diagram is the existence of only little order; that is, a weak relationship between the two variables. To the extent that such a relationship does exist, it appears to be found in the range of small distances. When this range is ignored, no order at all seems to prevail. Table 6.1 serves to pursue this line of investigation.

For ease of presentation and drawing inferences, the universe of 4,629 observations is classified into 20 ranges of distances of 1,000 km each, from the first of 0–999 km to the last of 19,000–19,999 km. The number of observations in each distance range is recorded in Column (2), the aggregate size of trade in each distance-range in Column (3), and the average size of each trade flow within the range in Column (4). The relationship of the latter (average flow) to distance (range) is also presented by means of Chart 6.2.

Several inferences suggest themselves. First, a (negative) relationship of the size of a trade flow between partners to their distance from each other does exist. This is less than a surprise. But two important qualifications of this rule stand out. First, while a trend (of the relationship) does exist, fluctuations around the trend line are major.[9] Thus, the relationship is highly irregular.

---

similar set of observations of exports. In fact, needless to say, data are not perfect. The mirror is thus slightly distorted, but not in any meaningful way. In the study we present only the analysis of export flows. But we made sure, in a parallel analysis not presented here, that the use of a set of observations for imports yields basically the same inferences.

[9] These fluctuations cannot be explained by erratic changes originating from a small number of observations which include some unusual and extreme records; observations in each of the distance ranges, except for the highest, number in the hundreds.

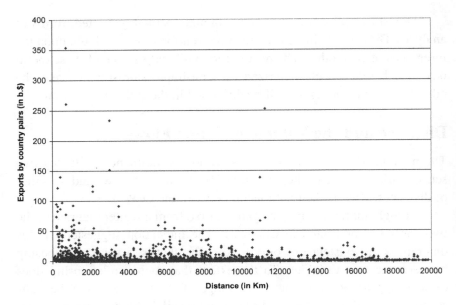

Chart 6.1:   Distance and trade flows

Table 6.1:   Distance range and trade flows

Distance Range (in km) (1)			No. of Observations (2)	Aggregate Exports (in b.$) (3)	Average Exports (in b.$) ((3)/(2)) (4)
1	0	999	369	3,309	8.96
2	1,000	1,999	670	1,977	2.95
3	2,000	2,999	430	916	2.13
4	3,000	3,999	349	986	2.82
5	4,000	4,999	310	366	1.18
6	5,000	5,999	260	803	3.09
7	6,000	6,999	201	745	3.70
8	7,000	7,999	226	501	2.22
9	8,000	8,999	303	533	1.75
10	9,000	9,999	374	376	1.00
11	10,000	10,999	290	521	1.80
12	11,000	11,999	223	486	2.18

Table 6.1:   (*Continued*)

Distance Range (in km) (1)			No. of Observations (2)	Aggregate Exports (in b.$) (3)	Average Exports (in b.$) ((3)/(2)) (4)
13	12,000	11,999	120	80	0.67
14	13,000	13,999	95	65	0.68
15	14,000	14,999	83	79	0.55
16	15,000	15,999	84	147	1.75
17	16,000	16.999	77	134	1.74
18	17,000	17,999	66	29	0.44
19	18,000	18,999	48	9	0.19
20	19,999	19,000	31	30	0.97
All observations			4,629	12,095	2.61
Excluding range (1)			4,260	8,786	2.06
Range (1)			369	3,309	8.96

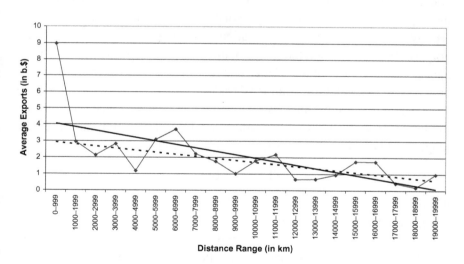

Chart 6.2:   Distance range and trade flows

More importantly, the relationship is weak, in comparison with expectations of the conventional wisdom. For instance, sizes of the average trade flows read from the solid trend line in Chart 6.2 tell us that moving from a distance of 1,000–1,999 km (a mid-point of 1,500 km) to the distance of 7,000–7,999 km (a midpoint 7,500 km) — that is, multiplying distance by five-fold — would lower the trade flow by just 35%, whereas a unit elasticity of trade to distance would predict the reduction of trade by as much as 80%.

Second, an inference which clearly suggests itself is the overwhelming impact of trade within the shortest distance range on any overall trend of the trade–distance relationship. Within the first range category, that of 0–999 km, some 27% of aggregate world trade is conducted, and the size of the average trade flow within this distance range is far higher than at any other range. The impact of trade flows within this shortest range must thus be of major importance for general rules which are found to characterize the relationship of trade to distance. The exclusion of transactions conducted within just this range must weaken — probably crucially so — the apparent relationship of trade to distance. In Figure 2 the dashed line represents the trend line of this relationship, when the first distance category (0–999 km) is excluded from the universe of observations. This appears to be a substantially flatter line representing a weaker relationship between distance and the volume of trade.

We add to these findings by estimating the trade–distance relationship in the universe of observations (rather than by classification into distance ranges). This relationship is estimated by the simple regression:

$$T_{jk} = \alpha + \beta D_{jk}$$

where

j, k are two trade partners;

T_{jk} is the size of the trade flow; and

D_{jk} is the great circle distance in kilometers between the two trade partners.

The outcome is presented in Table 6.2. From line (1), it is first seen that the relationship of the two variables is weak; the R^2 of the equation is very low. The coefficient of the trade–distance relationship appears to

Table 6.2: Relationship of trade flows to distance

	No. of Observation (1)	Adj R^2 (2)	t Value (3)	Distance Coefficient (4)
a. All observations	4609	0.073	−19.11	−0.852
b. Distance above 2500 km	3563	0.002	−2.79	−0.249

Dependent Variable = log value of exports; independent variable = log distance.

be high, at −0.852; but just the exclusion of the lowest distance range (0–999 km) lowers the coefficient to −0.249 as well as lowering the R^2 to practically zero.

The particularly strong (relatively speaking) relationship of trade to distance at the lowest range of the latter raises an important issue. Suppose countries in this distance range amongst them are not only close (by definition) to each other but also large in their trade volumes. A sizable trade between each such pair of countries may be expected regardless of distance, arising simply from the fact that the potential partner is a heavy trader. The estimated trade–distance relationship would thus yield a misleading inference. This is not just a hypothetical suggestion; very important segments of geographically–close nations are particularly large trading nations — primarily in Europe, but also in North America.

The next section will employ a method of inquiry which would free the investigation from the impact of the size of the trading partner, thus revealing purely the relationship between distance and trade flows.[10] We now move to it.

Distance and Trade Intensity

The basic measure for the study of trade–distance relationship in the following is the well-known "intensity ratio":

$$IR_{jk}^x = \frac{X_{jk}}{X_j} \bigg/ \frac{M_k}{M_w}$$

---

[10]This is obviously addressed in the "gravity model", in which "mass" is separated from distance. But the method we use is entirely different.

where, j, k are two trade partners (j is the home country)

IR_{jk}^{x} is the intensity ratio of j's exports to k;

X_{jk} = volume of j's exports to k;

$X_{\cdot j}$ = aggregate volume of j's exports;

$M_{\cdot k}$ = aggregate volume of k's imports; and

M_{w} = aggregate volume of world imports[11]

A ratio of unity would tell us that the share of country j's exports to partner k out of j's aggregate exports is identical to the share of partner k in aggregate world imports; that is, that the size of this trade flow is "explained" by the weight of the partner in world imports. This would thus be an expression of "neutrality" in the trade relationship at hand, with no bias involved. A ratio below unity would represent a negative bias and a ratio above unity — a positive bias.[12] "Bias" has, in this context, no normative connotation; it is just the expression of the tendency of one country to trade with a partner differently from what the sheer size of the latter as a trader would call for. That is, it reflects the existence of factors other than the size (in trade) of a partner which participate in determining the size of a trade flow with a partner.

A variety of such factors would suggest themselves. The salient ones mostly are mentioned in "gravity-model" analyses. An obvious factor that comes to mind is distance, the element to which the present analysis is mostly addressed. Thus, the question we pose is this: to what extent may the (positive or negative) "bias" in trade flows among partners be explained by distance[13] among them?

Space limitations do not allow the full presentation of the matrix of export intensity ratios here, nor for the matrix of bilateral distances. Instead, Chart 6.3, similarly to Chart 6.1 earlier, presents a scatter diagram of the relationship of distance to the intensity ratio in trade.

---

[11] Strictly speaking, not M_{w} but $M_{w}-M_{\cdot k}$ should appear in the denominator — excluding country k's own imports from world imports. But applying this qualification would make the estimation work much more complicated, and would matter little. For most trading nations the correction would be negligible. For the few large ones in which it is not, it would still be of minor importance.

[12] In fact, the intensity ratio may not be expected to be unity, except in rare cases.

[13] These may be obtained from the authors upon request.

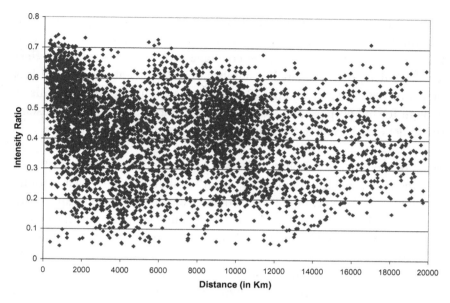

Chart 6.3: Distance and trade intensity

Table 6.3: Relationship of trade intensity to distance

	No. of Observations (1)	Adj R² (2)	t Value (3)	Distance Coefficient (4)
a. All observations	4690	0.050	−15.78	−0.094
b. Distance below 2500 km	1076	0.031	−5.97	−0.106
c. Distance above 2500 km	3614	0.000	−0.81	−0.009
d. Data for 1963	1722	0.069	−11.30	−0.117

Dependent variable = log export intensity ratio; independent variable = log distance.

The visual inference from the chart is clear cut; (1) to the extent that there is any relationship of the intensity of trade to distance, it must be weak; and (2) that such a relationship might perhaps be stronger for trade flows conducted within relatively short distances than for trade flows conducted within longer distances (this obviously agrees with a similar inference suggested earlier). We now turn to the formal analysis of such hypotheses.

Table 6.3 presents the findings of a simple regression analysis in which the intensity ratio of a trade flow is explained by the distance between the two partners to the flow. To add some perspective, we also present in the table (row d) the outcome of a similar procedure applied to trade data of 1963. Naturally, the coverage of the latter is narrower than the 2008 data, due to a smaller number of independent nations and less inclusive data coverage; only 43 countries are represented. But this is enough for the purpose at hand, particularly since almost all the substantial traders are included. Several inferences emerge from the findings.

(1) For the universe of observations, a rather weak relationship between the two variables is indicated: the R^2 is about 0.050 — that is, quite low. The elasticity of the size of trade to changes in distance appears to be roughly −0.09.[14] This is radically different from the unit elasticities (or above) found by the recorded "gravity equation" analyses. To the extent that it is meaningful, this elasticity should be in conformity with the levels of transportation costs referred to earlier.

(2) The relationship between the two variables improves somewhat when observations are confined to the range below 2,500 km. The R^2 remains low, at 0.031, but the elasticity of trade to distance increases slightly to close to −0.11. For the range of distances above 2,500 km, on the other hand, the relationship between the two variables practically disappears.[15] This, again, would conform with the observation made earlier about the presumably low level of marginal (to distance) costs. The indications provided by Table 6.3 are, thus, not surprising.

(3) The salient findings represent, most probably, fundamental, long-term structures of trade. The estimated coefficients for 1963 (row d) are very close to those of 2008 (row a). A thorough investigation of changes over time would obviously require more than the analysis presented here. Yet, it would seem unlikely that major fluctuations (of the relevant coefficients) took place, back and forth, during the decades between the early 1960s and the end of the first decade of the 21st century.

---

[14] It should be easy to see that the elasticity of the size of a trade flow is identical to the elasticity of the trade's intensify ratio.

[15] We have experimented with classifying distances into other ranges than below or above 2,500 km but the outcomes seemed to be less meaningful.

Distance Joined with Other Explanatory Variables

Apart from distance, several other factors may be expected to have an impact on the "bias" in the direction of trade flows. We shall now add them to the analysis. The first two such attributes are well known and, as we have mentioned earlier, have been widely explored in the literature. These are:

a. **Shared borders of the two partner countries to a trade flow.** Not much needs to be said about this: both a-priori expectation and much research have pointed to its significance in expanding trade between potential partners.

b. **Shared cultures, histories, and institutions.** Once more, a-priori reasoning would certainly assign significance to these attributes in expanding bilateral trade flows. Empirical research is, in this case, less feasible, since these attributes cannot easily be quantified and measured. Mostly, they are represented by the existence of just one attribute, namely, a common language between the two partners.

These two variables are clearly related to distance, and are expected to be manifested the closer the two partners to each other. For shared borders, this holds almost by definition;[16] but the relationship must also be strong when cultural affinities (represented by a common language) are concerned. Hence, the explicit addition of these two variables to the analysis should serve to weaken the apparent relationship of trade intensities to distance. In fact, though, while pointing out the relevance of these attributes, their impact will not be shown in the following statistical analysis for a simple reason; the analysis attempted with their inclusion showed no relationship of the two to trade intensities. This may be due to their small representation; among over 4,500 observations, those which encompass shared borders or common language amount only to a few hundreds each.

We are thus left with two other variables, which are less commonly addressed, and which hence deserve a few words of explanation. It should

---

[16] If the two partners have large territories (say, the USA and Canada, or Russia and China), this slightly weakens the association of "distance" (as measured) and shared borders.

be observed that both these variables are not expected to be related to distance on a-priori grounds.

c. **Trade compatibility.** Trade between two potential partners may be expected to be higher the more one partner has to offer of what the other partner demands. This matching of desires and offers may be viewed through the compatibility of trade structures, namely, the more one potential partner exports goods which loom large in the other partner's import structure, ceteris paribus, the more the two nations should trade with each other. In the extreme (negative) case, when one partner exports none of the goods which the other imports, no trade between the two should be expected. On the other extreme, trade would be maximized when the export structure of one partner is identical with the other's import structure. This relationship of the export–import structures of the two potential partners is represented by the index of compatibility of trade structures. The index is defined as follows:[17]

$$CM_{jk} = 1 - \frac{\sum_i \left| \frac{X_{ij}}{X_{\cdot j}} - \frac{M_{jk}}{M_{\cdot k}} \right|}{2}$$

where

    j and k are two trade partners;

    X_{ij} = exports of good i by country j;

    $X_{\cdot j}$ = aggregate exports of j;

    M_{ij} = imports of good i by country k; and

    $M_{\cdot k}$ = aggregate imports of country k.

d. **Similarity of income levels.** There are several reasons why similarity, or absence thereof, of the income levels of two potential partners should be a factor which participates in determining the size of trade between them, but two basic considerations point in opposite directions. Per-capita income levels represent, by and large (with some notable exceptions), levels of development and indicators of

---

[17] The index of compatibility is presented in several of Michaely's writings. The latest is in Ch. 9 of Michaely (2009).

structures of economies. Disparity in income levels should thus be related to dissimilarity of economic structures; and, in particular, of relative scarcity or abundance, of relative prices, and of factors of production — in particular of natural resources and unskilled labor vs. capital and skilled labor. The larger this disparity, the larger the "Heckscher-Ohlin" type of trade between the partners should be. On the other hand, the more similar the two economies, the more should the demand patterns of the two be compatible, and, for by now well-known reasons, the stronger the intra-industry trade flows between the two. Due to this ambiguity, it is not certain, on a-priori grounds, whether similarity of income levels should be a positive or a negative factor in determining the size of trade flows between partners. But since it might be an important element, one way or another, its inclusion among the explanatory variables of trade intensity seems to be warranted.

The degree of dissimilarity between the income levels is defined simply as

$$\left|GDP_j^c - GDP_k^c\right|;$$

that is, as the (absolute) difference between per–capita products in the two economies.

The relationship between the intensity ratio in trade (exports) and the three explanatory variables (distance, compatibility, and dissimilarity of income levels) is formulated by:

$$Log\left(I_{jk}^x\right) = \alpha + \lambda Log\left(D_{jk}\right) + \beta Log\left(Sx_j m_k\right) + \gamma Log\left(\left| GDP_j^c - GDP_k^c \right|\right),$$

where:

j, k are two trade partners (j is the home country);

I_{jk}^x is the intensity ratio of j's exports to k;

D_{jk} is the great circle distance in kilometers between the two trade partners;

$Sx_j m_k$ is the Index of compatibility of exports of country j and imports of country k; and

Table 6.4: Trade intensity and explanatory variables

Variable (1)	Parameter Estimate (2)	t Value (3)
a. Exports		
No. of observation = 4609; Adj R^2 = 0.167		
Intercept	−0.713	−11.05
Distance	−0.028	−4.64
Compatibility	0.066	25.17
Income differential	0.012	2.91
b. Imports		
No. of observations = 4646; Adj R^2 = 0.160		
Intercept	−0.065	−10.15
Distance	−0.037	−6.18
Compatibility	0.069	24.14
Income differential	0.013	3.23

$\left|GDP_j^C - GDP_k^C\right|$ is the absolute difference between per–capita products in the two economies.

The estimation is applied to the <u>log</u> form of the variables. The coefficients λ, β, γ, constitute the elasticities of the trade flow to changes in the respective explanatory variables. The findings are presented in Table 6.4. Several salient inferences may be drawn from these findings:

First, despite the addition of other explanatory variables, all of these together offer only a minor explanation of the level of intensity ratios; the adjusted R^2 appears to be only around 0.16.

Second, the elasticity of trade to distance appears to be, as might be expected, even lower than in the absence of other (than distance) explanatory variables; it appears now to be at the level of −0.03 to −0.04.

Third, the elasticity of trade to the level of compatibility of respective trade flows appears to be higher than that applying to distance — around 0.07 (the t values are much higher here as well). This implies that, in explaining the intensity of trade between two potential partners, the structures of their (aggregate) trade flows should not be ignored.

Fourth, dissimilarities in income levels of two partners seem to have a positive impact on the intensity of their mutual trade. But it is weak. The interpretation of this finding when it is this low is not clear-cut, since it presumably reflects, as has been discussed before, the net impact of contradictory (in sign) effects of the variable at hand on mutual trade.

Summary and Conclusions

The "conventional wisdom" perception of the relationship between geographical distance and trade flows among potential partners, based on a large number of empirical findings drawn from gravity analyses, is that distance has a strong impact on trade: typically, the elasticity estimates of trade to distance found in these studies run around unity. This stands in stark contrast to estimates of transportation costs, which imply that increasing distances should add only little to price. The present study examines directly the trade–distance relationship, to try to see whether the "conventional wisdom" may not be mistakenly held.

The study encompasses around 70 countries, with over 4,500 bilateral trade flows among them. It uses two alternative forms of analysis. One is the observation of the relationship between trade and distance yielded directly by data of trade flows. The other is based on "intensity ratios" of trade, and asks to what extent distance may explain the "bias" in mutual trade relationships — that is, the extent to which the size of a trade flow differs from what would be derived from a "neutral" assumption that the specific trade flow is just a function of aggregate trade volumes of the two potential partners.

Both methods yield similar inferences. These are:

First, a (negative) relationship between bilateral trade flows and bilateral distances does exist — it would be highly surprising if it did not. But this relationship appears to be weak, far from the strength expected from commonly–accepted estimates. This finding does agree with observations of transportation costs being, by and large, a quite minor component of prices in world trade.

Second, the relationship at hand tends to be somewhat stronger when relatively short distances are examined; it also tends to almost vanish over long distances. This, once more, agrees with the presumption that marginal transportation costs are substantially lower than average costs; it would also be compatible with the assumption that "distance" represents factors other than measurable transportation costs, such as (vaguely defined) "information costs", similarity among partners of legal systems, institutions, commercial rules, or cultural ties. All these potential elements would presumably exist between close neighbors, but they should not change much when gradually rising distances are concerned.

Third, among other factors (besides distance) which might explain the strength (or weakness) of trade ties between potential partners, the compatibility of export and import structures between any pair of countries — the degree to which one's exports structure (hence export supply) is similar to the other's import structure (hence import demand) — suggests itself as a significant element.

Intuition tells us that the size of trade flows between partners is influenced (negatively) by their distance from each other. Not surprisingly, this expectation is borne out by the findings of the present study: an impact of distance on trade does exist. Like the proverbial Old Soldiers, distance is not dead; it just fades away. The impact of distance appears to be weak, far weaker than prior studies would have led us to believe. By and large, distance does not appear to be a dominant factor in determining trade flows among nations. It largely loses relevance beyond a fairly short range.

It is always tempting — indeed, almost a methodological imperative — to try to explain phenomena and relationships in the context of a coherent model. The "gravity equation" does perform this task. But one of its principal findings — concerning the impact of distance — appears to be in doubt. The present study does not presume to suggest an alternative model. Its findings do imply, however, that the analysis of relationships of trade flows among nations requires additional components, which apparently outweigh by far the impact of distance. Some of these may probably best be assembled under the designation of "history"; that is, phenomena and attributes which must have been important in the past and whose impact persists today, though they may no longer exist now nor feasibly be quantified and estimated.

Annex 6-A: Trade Patterns of Small Countries

In discussions with colleagues, two issues which might have influenced our inferences have been raised. One is the possibility that by excluding from the study very small countries (in size of trade) we may have introduced a bias; that the impact of distance on trade patterns of small countries may be different from that prevalent in the larger ones. The other issue: our observations involve only positive trade flows; hence, they ignore the possibility that distance may have a consistent impact on the complete absence of trade among nations, and ignoring this potential may have biased our inferences.

The present annex will be devoted to the first issue; namely, it will investigate the trade flows of very small countries. The next, Annex 6-B, will address the second, the potential impact of distance on the complete absence of trade. In a basic sense, the trade flows of very small countries are of minor consequence for the observation of world trade. The aggregate trade of countries excluded (due to size) from the main body of this study amounts, roughly, to just one tenth of aggregate world trade. Thus, this trade should have only minor implications for inferences regarding global trade patterns. But it may still be of some use to explore the possibility that trade patterns of very small countries (which we shall refer to as "ultra-small") differ, where the impact of distance is involved, from those of their large partners.

Off-hand, it does not appear on a-priori grounds that the relationship between trade flows and distance of partners should be consistently different — one way or another — in trade of small vs larger partners. Casual impressions of trade patterns do not suggest such bias either. But we shall not be content with such observations and shall pursue here a more rigorous analysis.

This will be done by following a similar procedure to the one practiced in the main body of the study. First, we identify 71 "ultra-small" countries.[18] In principle, we include here all 107 world countries which

---

[18] In this context, they are "small" in terms of trade flows. In other attributes (population, territory) they may often be quite large (Ethiopia or Vietnam may serve as extreme examples).

are not covered in the main study. But, as might be expected, the required data (that is, data for both trade flows and distance) are often missing. These 71 "ultra-small" countries will be our group of reference.[19] For convenience, we shall refer to the countries included in the main study as "large", though they range from some that are very large indeed (the USA, Germany) to many which are pretty small (in terms of their shares in world trade). The intensity ratios of trade between each ultra-small and each large country (once more, for exports) will be estimated; and then, related to distance between each pair of countries.

Altogether, close to 3,500 observations are recorded (3,489 to be precise). This is a sufficiently large number for drawing solid inferences — certainly of the nature we look for here — and the outcome of the analysis is indeed clear cut. A regression analysis (of the export intensity ratio over distance) yields the following coefficients:

AD_j $R^2 = 0.020$
Regression coefficient $= -0.001$
t value $= -8.47$.

The outcome is obviously highly significant, and it shows practically no relationship between the intensity of trade and the distances among trading partners. This is even a much stronger finding than that of the main study in which such a relationship, though pretty weak, does exist. The salient inference, for our purpose, is that the estimated impact of distance on trade indicated in the main body of the study could <u>not</u> be biased downwards by the exclusion from the study of "ultra-small" countries. If anything, this exclusion must have led to an upward bias of the impact of distance on trade patterns.

---

[19] The group includes: Armenian, Aruba, Bahamas, Belize, Benin, Bhutan, Bolivia, Bosnia-Herzegovina, Botswana, Burkina Paso, Burundi, Cambodia, Cameroon, Central Africa Rep., Comoros, Congo, Dominica, Dominican Rep., El Salvador, Ethiopia, Faeroe Islands, Fiji, French Polynesia, Gabon, Gambia, Georgia, Ghana, Grenada, Guatemala, Guinea, Jamaica, Jordan, Kiribati, Kyrgyzstan, Latvia, Lebanon, Madagascar, Malawi, Mali, Malta, Mauritania, Mauritius, Mayotte, Mozambique, Namibia, Netherland Antilles, New Caledonia, Nicaragua, Niger, Panama, Paraguay, Rwanda, St. Kitts and Nevis, Santa Lucia, St. Vincent and the Grenadines, Samoa, St. Tome and Principe, Senegal, Seychelles, Solomon Islands, Sri Lanka, Surinam, Togo, Tonga, Uganda, Uruguay, Vietnam, Yemen, Zambia, and Zimbabwe.

Annex 6-B: Distance and the Absence of Trade

An exploration of the potential impact of distance on the complete absence of trade among potential partners requires some deviation from the conventional estimation of elasticities. If a change in one (the explanatory) variable leads to the reduction of the other (the explained one) to zero, the presumed elasticity is infinite. But this is not of much relevance: all elasticities in such cases would be infinite, regardless of the extent of the impact of one variable on the other. And, of no less importance, the inclusion of any such individual case within a "basket" or a group would make the elasticity of the relationship at hand infinite for the whole group, regardless of the weight of the item concerned in the group (as long as it is positive). Hence, some alternative method of estimating the potential impact of distance on the <u>absence</u> of trade must be devised. We suggest here one such approximation.

Similar to the procedure in the main study, we construct a matrix of bilateral trade flows among each pair of countries. But instead of recording the size of trade (the "intensity ratio"), we use a binary classification: a "zero" if trade in this "box" is completely absent; and "one" when some trade does take place. Alongside with this, we record the distance between the countries involved. In each box of the matrix two magnitudes are thus recorded: "zero" or "one", and distance. The assembly of all observations in all the boxes will then provide a series of the association of the two variables: distance and absence (or existence) of trade. A regression of the "zero-one" recorded observation on the recorded distance should thus yield an <u>elasticity</u> of the relationship of the two — different from the conventional one but an "elasticity" nevertheless.

Altogether, over 4,500 "boxes", or units of observation, are constructed. A presentation of the full matrix would obviously not be feasible here. Instead, we present a summary table in which all observations are classified (in the same manner as in Table 6.5) into groups of distance, 1,000 km each (0–999; 1,000–1,999; etc.). These groups are presented in Column (1) of Table 6.B.1, Column (2) of the table records, for information, the number of observations ("boxes") in each distance category; whereas Column (3) presents the (unweighted) mean of the frequency of "zero" trade in each distance category.

The impression gained from this presentation is of the existence of a large variance among the groups; but no consistent relationship of frequency of "zeroes" to distance is apparent. Based thus on such impression, no clear impact of geographic distance on the existence or absence of trade flows among potential partners is indicated.

Annex Table 6.B.1: Frequency of absence of trade ("zeroes"), by distance

Distance Range (kms)	Number of Observations	Frequency (in Percent)
1–999	348	23.4
1000–1999	634	24.5
2,000–2,999	428	17.5
3,000–3,999	358	12.5
4,000–4,999	310	8.5
5,000–5,999	262	7.5
6,000–6,999	204	6.1
7,000–7,999	224	6.7
8,000–8,999	304	8.9
9,000–9,999	372	13.7
10,000–10,999	284	12.6
11,000–11,999	220	11.2
12,000–12,999	120	6.5
13,000–13,999	98	5.9
14,000–14,999	86	7.3
15,000–15,999	82	9.4
16,000–16,999	78	9.9
17,000–17,999	64	11.1
18,000–18,000	48	16.1
19,000 and upwards	32	22.5

We now move to a more rigorous analysis. A regression analysis of the two variables (the dependent variable being the frequency of "zeroes" and the independent being distance), involving all (over 4,500) observations, yields the following:

Adj R^2 = 0.010;

Regression coefficient = 0.073; and

t value = −20.42.

The estimated "elasticity" of this dependence is thus close to zero. In addition, as the size of the coefficient of variance indicated, distance plays practically no role in explaining the frequency of "zeroes". A strong conclusion thus emerges; the complete absence of trade among potential partners is <u>not</u> a function of distances among partners.

Annex Table to Chapter 6:   Shares in world exports — 2008

(In percent of world exports: in descending order)

(Total world exports = 16,117 b.$)

Country	Share	Cumulative	Country	Share	Cumulative
1. Germany	8.97	8.97	17. Spain	1.75	65.89
2. China	8.88	17.85	18. Taipei	1.59	67.48
3. USA	7.99	25.84	(Chinese)*		
4. Japan	4.85	30.69	19. U. Arab Emirate	1.48	68.96
5. Netherlands	3.96	34.65	20. Switzerland	1.24	70.20
6. France	3.82	38.47	21. Malaysia	1.24	71.44
7. Italy	3.37	41.84	22. Brazil	1.23	72.67
8. Belgium	2.93	44.77	23. India	1.21	73.88
9. Russia	2.93	47.69	24. Australia	1.16	75.04
10. UK	2.85	50.55	25. Sweden	1.14	76.18
11. Canada	2.83	53.38	26. Austria	1.13	77.30
12. Rep. of Korea	2.62	56.00	27. Thailand	1.10	78.41
13. Hong Kong	2.30	58.29	28. Norway	1.07	79.48
(China)			29. Poland	1.06	80.54
14. Singapore	2.10	60.39	30. Czech Rep.	0.91	81.45
15. Saudi Arabia*	1.94	62.34	31. Indonesia	0.87	82.31
16. Mexico	1.81	64.15	32. Turkey	0.82	83.13

(Continued)

Annex Table to Chapter 6:   *(Continued)*

Country	Share	Cumulative	Country	Share	Cumulative
33. Ireland	0.78	83.91	58. Colombia	0.23	95.11
34. Denmark	0.72	84.64	59. Slovenia	0.21	95.33
35. Iran, Islamic Rep.*	0.71	85.34	60. Belarus	0.20	95.53
36. Hungary	0.67	86.01	61. Peru	0.20	95.72
37. Finland	0.60	86.61	62. Azerbaijan	0.19	95.91
38. Venezuela	0.59	87.20	63. New Zealand	0.19	96.10
39. Kuwait	0.54	87.74	64. Egypt	0.16	96.26
40. Nigeria	0.51	88.25	65. Greece	0.16	96.42
41. South Africa	0.50	88.75	66. Luxembourg	0.16	96.58
42. Algeria	0.49	89.25	67. Lithuania	0.15	96.73
43. Kazakhstan	0.44	89.69	68. Bulgaria	0.14	96.87
44. Slovak Rep.	0.44	90.13	69. Pakistan	0.13	96.99
45. Argentina	0.43	90.56	70. Morocco	0.13	97.12
46. Ukraine	0.42	90.98	71. Tunisia	0.12	97.24
47. Chile	0.41	91.39	72. Trinidad & Tob*	0.12	97.36
48. Angola*	0.40	91.79	73. Ecuador	0.11	97.47
49. Libya*	0.39	92.18	74. Bahrain*	0.11	97.58
50. Vietnam	0.39	92.57	75. Equat. Guinea*	0.10	97.68
51. Iraq*	0.39	92.95	76. Bangladesh*	0.10	97.78
52. Israel	0.38	93.34	77. Syria	0.09	97.86
53. Qatar	0.35	93.69	78. Croatia	0.09	97.95
54. Portugal	0.35	94.03	79. Estonia	0.08	98.03
55. Romania	0.31	94.34	80. Turkmenistan*	0.08	98.10
56. Philippines	0.30	94.64	81. Sudan*	0.07	98.17
57. Oman	0.23	94.88	82. Serbia	0.07	98.24

*Detailed trade data not available at the *COMTRADE* database.

Chapter 7

The Distance Level of Trade

Subject Matter and Method

We have seen, in the previous chapter, that distance between countries does <u>not</u> have a major impact on or explain much of the size of trade between potential trade partners. In view of this finding, we shall now ask: what is the <u>distance level</u> of a country's trade? That is, does the country tend to trade with nearby (geographically) countries or perhaps (counter to intuition) with faraway partners? Or, possibly, with no bias one way or another? To address this issue, we start by constructing an index of "the distance level" of a country's trade (as in most of the study, we shall refer to exports). We then, in turn, try to examine potential relationships of this level to what seem to be relevant attributes of the nature of an economy.

We start by estimating the distance level through the mean of the distance of the home country with a potential customer country; with any other country on the globe. This is a simple arithmetic mean, with no weight (i.e., with equal weights) assigned to any of the individual distances.

Designate:

j = Home country

k = Partner country

Dis_{kj} = Geographic distance (in kilometers) between j and k

$Dis._j$ = Mean distance level of j's trade

N = Number of countries (potential partners)

Then, the <u>near</u> distance of a country's trade is

$$\text{Dis}_{.j} = \frac{\sum \text{Dis.j.k}}{n}.$$

This is, thus, a given geographical attribute, which as such does not indicate country j's trade pattern. However, it is required for further exploration of this pattern. The level of this distance is indicated in column (1) of Table 7.1. As would intuitively be expected, a generally low distance

Table 7.1:   Distance level of exports (in km)

Country	Unweighted (1)	Export Weighted (2)	Ratio (2)/(1) (3)	Partner-Imports Weighted (4)	Ratio (4)/(1) (5)
Algeria	4774	3584	0.75	4821	1.01
Argentina	10872	7558	0.7	11706	1.08
Australia	11623	7843	0.67	13563	1.17
Austria	4439	1048	0.37	4597	1.04
Azerbaijan	5030	4265	0.85	4992	0.99
Belarus	4480	1576	0.35	4695	1.05
Belgium	4395	1434	0.33	4790	1.09
Czech (Rep.)	4388	1049	0.24	4637	1.06
Denmark	4359	1685	0.39	4777	1.10
Ecuador	9204	4497	0.49	10881	1.18
Egypt	5351	2952	0.55	5225	0.98
Estonia	4450	1353	0.31	4877	1.10
Finland	4461	2395	0.54	4923	1.10
France	4468	2185	0.49	4929	1.10
Germany	4366	2189	0.49	4785	1.10
Greece	4883	1844	0.38	4784	0.98
Hungary	4488	1256	0.28	4580	1.02
India	6124	4900	0.8	6775	1.11
Indonesia	8820	6302	0.71	10074	1.14
Ireland	4567	2715	0.59	5244	1.14

Table 7.1: *(Continued)*

Country	Unweighted (1)	Export Weighted (2)	Ratio (2)/(1) (3)	Partner-Imports Weighted (4)	Ratio (4)/(1) (5)
Israel	5259	5404	1.02	5131	0.97
Italy	4679	2386	0.51	4770	1.02
Japan	6923	6137	0.89	9285	1.34
Kazakhstan	5450	3476	0.64	6109	1.12
Korea (Rep.)	6444	4907	0.76	8523	1.32
Lithuania	4448	1403	0.32	4698	1.06
Luxembourg	4381	939	0.21	4738	1.08
Malaysia	8034	5536	0.69	9274	1.68
Mexico	8254	3713	0.45	10592	1.28
Morocco	5346	3465	0.65	5717	1.07
Netherlands	4368	1467	0.34	4867	1.11
New Zealand	12570	8687	0.69	14967	1.19
Nigeria	6798	6045	0.89	6856	1.13
Norway	4405	1791	0.41	4955	1.12
Oman	6066	3527	0.58	6332	1.04
Pakistan	5812	4935	0.85	6423	1.11
Peru	9932	7358	0.74	11482	1.16
Philippines	7787	5919	0.76	9614	1.23
Poland	4415	1347	0.31	4631	1.05
Portugal	5143	1934	0.38	5596	1.09
Qatar	5748	5230	0.91	5838	1.02
Romania	4660	1551	0.33	4639	1.00
Russian Fed.	4594	2051	0.45	4920	1.07
Serbia	4483	1438	0.32	4676	1.04
Singapore	8212	4219	0.51	9521	1.16
Slovak Rep.	4445	1096	0.25	4590	1.03
Slovenia	4489	958	0.21	4632	1.03
South Africa	8796	7816	0.89	8827	1.00
Spain	4918	2161	0.46	5306	1.08

(Continued)

Table 7.1:   *(Continued)*

Country	Unweighted (1)	Export Weighted (2)	Ratio (2)/(1) (3)	Partner-Imports Weighted (4)	Ratio (4)/(1) (5)
Sweden	4409	2401	0.54	4878	1.11
Syria	5027	1681	0.33	5069	1.01
Thailand	7394	5387	0.73	8834	1.19
Tunisia	4942	1602	0.32	4929	1.00
Turkey	4933	2256	0.46	4845	0.98
Ukraine	4560	1787	0.39	4568	1.00
Un. Arab Emirates	5958	1868	0.31	4690	0.79
UK	4441	2755	0.62	6074	1.37
USA	6416	5604	0.87	5000	0.89
Venezuela	8147	1868	0.23	9758	1.29
Viet Nam	7657	6797	0.89	9069	1.18

level is indicated for European countries, reflecting the short geographic distance among the (many) members of this area. On the other hand, generally high distance levels are shown for the geographically peripheral countries in Latin America or in East and Southeast Asia.

We now move to a measure of the distance level which <u>does</u> reflect the trade of a given country. It will be determined by the country's allocation of its trade (in our measurement exports) among all potential partners. Thus, individual distances will not be given equal weight but will be assigned a weight according to the allocation of the home-country's trade among the potential partners

Let

X_{jk} = Exports of (home) country j to (partner) country k; and
$X_{j.}$ = Aggregate exports of country j.

Designate:

Dis_j^x = Export-weighted mean distance level of country j.

Thus,

$$Dis_j^x = \sum_k \frac{X_{jk}}{X_{j.}} Dis_{jk}.$$

The estimated levels of this index of distance are presented in Column (2) of Table 7.1. One observation which stands out immediately, even without further analysis, is a glaring distinction between European countries and others. One could practically draw a line, below which almost all countries are part of Europe and, similarly, above which practically all countries belong to "the rest of the world". To make this observation more precise, we divide the universe of countries into two (exclusive) groups: "Europe" (26 countries) and "the rest of the world" (42 countries).[1] For the universe of (68) countries, the median level of the distance is 5055km; for just Europe, it is 4590km; for the rest of the world, the median is 6658km. Even more important, Europe's countries are almost homogenous, in this respect, with very little variation; almost all congregate around the median (the three slight deviations from this rule are Ireland and the two Iberian countries — perhaps not accidentally the three "peripheral" countries (in a territorial sense)). Even the highest-ranking distances in this group barely touch those at the lowest range in the other group. In the latter, the dispersion of distance levels is very large indeed, from, at the lowest, 4513km (for Ukraine) to 15,141km (for New Zealand. It thus appears that, for the purpose at hand, the world is practically divided into two separate trading zones: Europe vs. the rest of the world. We have encountered this distinction on earlier occasions, though not in such a clear-cut manner, and we shall have opportunities to refer to it again.

Column (3) of Table 7.1 presents the <u>ratio</u> of the "export weighted" and the "simple" levels to each other. In a most obvious way, the export-weighted distance level of a country's exports must have a close relationship to the unweighted (i.e., equally weighted) distance level. But the two are far from being equal. Moreover, a regularity of the relationship of the two indices to each other is clearly indicated by our observations. This appears unmistakably in column (3) of Table 7.1.

It appears that this ratio is universally below unity; the export-weighted distance level of exports is uniformly lower than the unweighted distance level. This finding holds for, in fact, the whole universe of the countries explored here.[2] Moreover, this ratio is overwhelmingly below

---

[1] "Europe" is defined, in this context, as continental Europe minus the "Former Soviet Union" countries and plus the island countries Ireland and the UK.

[2] The only exception, where the ratio of the two indices to each other is practically unity, is the case of Israel, a country for which trade with most of its neighbors is mostly precluded.

unity. The median level of the ratio is as low as 0.50; the weighted index of the distance level is just half of the unweighted level. This general observation should be explained in the following way. The export-weighted level is a function of two attributes, namely: the unweighted distance level and the geographic allocation of the country's exports. A below-unity ratio would then indicate that a tendency to direct the country's exports to <u>nearby</u> rather than faraway partners exists; that is, that distances have a negative impact on the geographic allocation of trade. By this evidence, thus, distance does have a negative influence on the geographic allocation of trade. We see no way of formally deriving a relationship between distance and the ratio at hand, but the intuitive inference from these findings is that the impact of distance is substantial.

But the observation of column (3) should not stop here. Even more than in our earlier analyses, it appears that the trade of European countries is radically different in the aspect at hand from that of other trading nations. The ratio is lower, overwhelmingly so, for European countries than for the rest. The ratio ranges for Europe[3] from 0.21 (for several countries) to: 0.62 (the UK). the <u>median</u> ratio for this group is <u>0.35</u> (in comparison, for 0.50 for the universe of 68 countries). For the ROW group the range is from 0.23 to 1.02. The median for this group is 0.71 — twice as high as the median (0.35) for the European group. It appears that for the ROW too distance does have an impact on the directions of trade flows of countries, but it must be substantially weaker than for members of the European group. This inference agrees fully with that which we have drawn in the earlier chapter, namely that distance has a meaningful impact on trade when <u>short</u> distances are involved, but that this impact tends to largely fade away when trade flows over large distances are compared.

We now move in a somewhat different direction. Thus far, we have regarded every single potential partner as a given unit, with all partners considered as equal, regardless of the partners' size. But this size (in terms

---

[3] It includes: Austria, Belarus, Bulgaria, Croatia, Czech. Rep., Denmark, Estonia, Finland, France, Germany, Greece, Hungary, Ireland, Italy, Lithuania, Luxembourg, Netherlands, Norway, Poland, Portugal, Romania, Russian Fed., Serbia, Slovak Rep., Slovenia, Spain, Sweden, Ukraine, and UK.

of trade) must be a crucial factor in determining the size of the home country's trade with the partner. To take this factor into account, we construct the following index.

Let,

Dis_{jk} = (as before) distance (in km) between (home) country j and (partner) country k;

$M_{\cdot k}$ = Aggregate <u>imports</u> of country k; and

M_w = Aggregate world imports[4]

Then:

$\text{Dis}_{kj}^M = \text{Dis}_{jk} \frac{M_{\cdot k}}{M_w}$ Partner-imports weighted distance between j and k; and

$$\text{Dis}_{kj}^M = \sum_k \left(\frac{X_{kj}}{X_{\cdot j}} \cdot \text{Dis}_{kj} \cdot \frac{M_{\cdot k}}{M_w} \right)$$

= Partner-imports weighted distance of country j's exports.[5]

The estimates of the partner's import weighed distance level for each of the 68 countries are presented in column (4) of Table 7.1.

Unlike the comparison of the indices presented in columns (1) and (2) (with their ratio expressed in column (3)), in the present instance we see no <u>a-priori</u> reason why the index presented in column (4) should generally exceed or fall short of the index presented in column (1) (the "unweighted" level); in moving from one index to the other, no pattern of <u>behavior</u> of the (home) country may be discerned. In fact, column (5) of Table 7.1 does indicate a slight deviation of the two indices of distance level: the import-weighted level is generally higher than the unweighted level. But the difference is slight; the median ratio is 1.091 with a heavy concentration

---

[4]As has been noted earlier on a similar occasion, the term M_w should, to be precise, be replaced by $M_w - M_k$; that is, aggregate world imports <u>excluding</u> the imports of country k itself. But, again as noted, making this refinement would require an elaborate work and, even when very large partners are involved, would not lead to any radical changes.

[5]The two elements which appear here, of geographic distance from the partner and of the partner's weight, appear also in the commonly used "gravity analysis", but the context here is entirely different.

around this level. That is, the import-weighted measure exceeds the unweighted one commonly by roughly one-tenth. We unfortunately have no ready-made explanation for this slight discrepancy. And we note, as a generalization, that adding the weight of trading partners does <u>not</u> contribute much to the estimation of distance level of trade.

Origins of Distance Level

In this final section, we try to analyze the issue: what are the factors which potentially lead to a high (or low) distance level of trade of an economy? We include in this exploration elements which intuitively suggest a potential impact on this level, in one direction or another. We first enumerate these elements, just indicating the reasons for which they may be of relevance; then, by conducting a statistical test, infer what the relevance of each element is.

First, and most obviously, must come the <u>geographic position</u> of a country, its being closer to, or far away from, all potential trading partners, i.e., to all countries in the rest of the world.

Next come two attributes (which must, in turn, be related to each other) of the <u>structure</u> of trade (in our exploration, of exports). One is the nature of the goods in which the economy specializes. It is conceivable that this nature — in particular, the degree to which the country's exports specialize in <u>resource-based vs. manufactured</u> products — affects the range of partners which are potentially appropriate customers for the country's exports. The other element is the level of <u>concentration</u> of the country's exports. Again, the degree to which the country exports many or just few goods is intuitively a factor in affecting the range of potential trade partners, which may in turn have an impact on the distance by which the country's trade travels.

Two other elements refer to the income level of the economy. One is the <u>per-capita income</u>, an indicator of the economy's richness or poorness. The other is the economy's <u>aggregate income,</u> an indicator of the country's economic size. Once more, both of these attributes might intuitively be guessed to have an impact on the range of the country's potential trade partners.

Table 7.2: Multiple-regression coefficients of distance level of exports and five contributing elements (2010 data)

Elements	Spearman Coefficient (1)	Pearson Coefficient (2)
1. Unweighted distance level	0.860	0.870
2. Ratio of manufacturing in export	−0.254	−0.264
3. (Gini-Hirschman) coefficient of concentration	0.304	0.124
4. The economy's <u>per-capita</u> GDP	−0.368	−0.264
5. The economy's aggregate GDP	−0.330	−0.327

All these five elements must be closely related, to one degree or another, to each other; this is intuitively clear, and has been formally indicated earlier in this study. Hence, a <u>multiple</u> regression test must be performed. The results of this procedure are presented in Table 7.2. Both the Spearman rank correlation coefficient and the Pearson coefficient are recorded — though, for reasons mentioned on other occasions in this study, we regard the former (rank correlation) coefficients to be the more appropriate measure for drawing inferences in the present context. (As it happens, though, the two sets of coefficients are very close to each other.) In this test, the "explained" variable is the <u>export-weighted</u> distance level of exports; and the "explanatory" variables are, in turn, each of the just-listed five elements.

With one slight exception (Pearson coefficient for level of concentration), all coefficients are significant at any desired level.

We now review the outcome of this test. First, the export-weighted distance level of exports is clearly related to the country's geographic position. This is obviously not surprising. What was less expected — to us, at least — is the <u>strength</u> of this relationship. With a correlation coefficient of 0.860, the simple (mean) geographic distance of a country from all other countries in the universe appears to have an overwhelming effect in determining the distance level of the country's trade. While, as we immediately indicate, all other tested elements are also relevant, they fade in importance in comparison with the impact of the country's geographic position.

All other four elements appear, indeed, to have significant impacts on the distance level in the directions which should have been expected a-priori. When the country's exports heavily consist of resource-based goods, the country's exports may presumably not be directed just to the (more natural) partners which lie nearby; a wider range of partners must be involved. This holds similarly for a country with highly-concentrated exports (note: the positive size of the coefficient in the Table is the outcome of the fact that the structural attribute is indicated by the index of concentration). These two attributes are, we often pointed out, clearly related to each other; yet, each appears to have an impact of its own. Finally, a rich (high per-capita income level) economy, which presumably tends to trade with similar economies, would not be commonly found to seek its main customer countries very far away. This holds true for economies of large size, whereas a small economy would tend to seek its partners relatively far away.

These findings may be summarized by observing the geographic location of a country. A country with a short distance level of trade would to a large extent be a European country: it lies close to potential customers; it is rich, with highly diversified exports; and it largely specializes in manufactured goods. In the other camp, of countries with large distance levels of trade, we more commonly find, for similar reasons but in the opposite direction, African countries, countries in South America and often Asian countries, particularly those in East and Southeast Asia.

Chapter 8

The Extent of Regional Trading

An A-Priori Assessment

"Regionalism" in trade may be defined in a variety of ways. One, which will not be followed here, is identified with policies: A set of policies adopted by a group of countries which are intended to bias trade of each of them toward partners to the group and away from others would define the group as a "region". While granting, as we shall do soon and through-out the text, an important role to policies in leading to "regionalism", the definition preferred here (as in most empirical studies) will refer to trade performance. That is, a region will be defined as a group of countries which tend to trade more with each other than with others.

In a general way, such a tendency may originate from a variety of sources. One has just been discussed: members of the "region" follow policies which grant preferences to trading with each other. Another is a set of "given" attributes, physical or otherwise, which lead to closer trade ties. These include geographical attributes, cultural attributes, institutional attributes such as a common language or legal structures, and historical patterns. Still another origin is the commodity structure of activities and trade of each country, even though these structures may themselves partly depend on the identity of the country's trade partners.

Over the short or medium run — time periods of several decades — the "given" attributes may indeed be viewed as predominantly unchanged so far as physical elements are concerned. Here too, however, their significance may change due to, for instance, changes in transportation costs. Commodity structures of activity and trade, on the other hand, may and do change over the medium term. Policies, needless to say, do change, and these changes do matter. In the present context, the major relevant policy instruments may be classified as follows:

(i) **Levels of trade barriers:** When these barriers (tariffs, NTBs) are uniform, they should have no a-priori impact on the tendency to trade with one category of countries or another; hence, (uniform) changes of such policy instruments should not lead to a move toward or away from regionalism in trade. But these levels do matter in an important way; the existence of barriers (this term standing for overall government instruments, including elements such as subsidies) is a necessary (not, of course, sufficient) condition for the introduction of preferential policies, as none of these may be introduced when trade is completely free. Similarly, the higher the general level of barriers, the larger the scope for and the potential impact of preferential policies.

(ii) **Preferential policies:** The existence of such policies does not indicate a tendency toward regional trading per se: preferences may be (and often are) granted on a bilateral basis, and thus are not biased towards (or against) regional trade flows. But multilateral preferential agreements are common, and these do contribute to the encouragement of regional trading. Thus, preferential policies do provide the general framework in which a scope for inducement of regional trade patterns exists.

(iii) **Inconvertibility of currencies:** Inconvertible (or less than fully convertible) currencies lead almost inevitably, though not by definition, to regional preferences. Differences in degrees of currency convertibility in a country's trade with its partners must introduce tendencies towards or away from its trading with different partners; these, in turn, commonly apply to groups rather than to individual partners. The "convertible sterling" of the early post-WWII era, granting a convertible currency to the conduct of trade only within the sterling area, was probably the classic example of such "regionally-convertible" currencies.

Salient Developments Over the Last Half-Century

Following this brief survey of the potential origins of regionalism and preceding the concrete estimates that will be suggested next, we may ask: what should be our a-priori expectation for the development of tendencies toward regionalism in trade over the last half-century?

(i) The "given" data — geography, cultural attributes, and so forth — have indeed been predominantly "given" and unchanged over the period. Some changes in political identities, or boundaries of countries did occur. But these were minor in terms of the relative sizes of trade which were involved — save, perhaps, the disintegration of the Soviet Union — and they do not indicate, commonly, an impact on the tendency toward regionalism in world trade one way or another.

(ii) Commodity patterns of trade have indeed changed over the period, often remarkably so. The exchange of primary goods of one partner with manufactures of the other has become less predominant and now constitutes only the minority of world trade (trade in oil being, at present, the major remaining component of this trade pattern). Intra-industry exchanges, on the other hand — "industry" being both narrowly defined or broadly classified, such as to "primary goods" and "manufactures" — have become more prominent. Whether this change by itself should lead toward or away from regionalism in trade is not a-priori obvious. It does lead, on the other hand, to an expectation that the identity of trading regions should have changed over this period.

(iii) Trade barriers have definitely changed, over the period, in an emphatic way. At the starting point, the world was probably more riddled with government intervention in trade than at any other point in the modern era, including over the decade of the 1930s. Toward the period's end, global trade became almost free, with only relatively minor intervention (save, perhaps, the agrarian sector). On this score, the potential for regional preferences contracted markedly. But two elements should be pointed out, working in the opposite direction. First, we note that some (definitely not all) barriers were removed, to start with, through regional preferential policies (the European Union (EU) being an obvious example). Second, the progress from just the removal of trade barriers to the introduction of measures of so-called "deep integration", such as the free movement of factors of production, coordination of legal or institutional structures, and harmonization of fiscal and monetary policies, was obviously conducted in regional frameworks. These measures should presumably lead to a particular expansion of regional trade (though the impact is not clear, on a-priori grounds, when freeing of labor movements is concerned). The outstanding example of this pattern is again the EU, under its various historical guises. In this context of removal of barriers, special attention should be paid to the radical change, over the period, in currency regimes, from a world of mostly inconvertible currencies to one with an almost free and universal world market for the large majority of currencies. This should certainly work to lower regional tendencies. Offsetting this may have worked for the adoption of common currencies, the introduction of the Euro being, once more, a prime example. But this element, it may be ventured, must have had a smaller impact than the global move to currency convertibility, including the disappearance of secluded areas of currency convertibility, such as the "convertible sterling".

Based on this a-priori survey of changing circumstances, it is not obvious whether an expansion or contraction of regionalism in trade should have been expected. What does seem clear is that the identity of trading regions must have changed radically over the period under review.

An Empirical Exploration of Regional Trading

The empirical analysis suggested here is [described as] tentative rather than a full-proof demonstration. This originates from the realization that "regionalism" may be expressed in a variety of forms, and that, in particular, the present exercise does not examine the movement from one set of "regions" to another which, as has been noted earlier, must have been important during the period under review. Moreover, the definition of "regions" must involve a high degree of arbitrariness. Nevertheless, I believe that on both scores the definition and classification of the specific "regions" suggested here provide a reasonable approach to at least an illustration of the magnitudes and development involved.

Definition of "Regions"

Any classification of sub-sections of the world as "regions" must involve a large degree of arbitrariness. At least three potential guiding rules for making this definition may be suggested.

(i) First, conventions of one sort or another may exist, based primarily on long-term patterns of trade. At present we do <u>not</u> seem to have such a historically commonly-applied conventional classification, hence, we must resort to other potential guidelines.

(ii) Second, "regions" may be defined by patterns of <u>policy.</u> Sets of policies which should lead to a bias in favor of trade flows within a group of countries would then make this group a "region". Given a plethora of preferential agreements, some of which being not much more than signed papers, it would not be fruitful to adhere to this guideline in a universal way. Only two sets of meaningful, comprehensive preferential agreements may be distinguished in the last half century. One is the set which applies to Western European countries, which has gradually developed into the present EU. The other applies to trade among the three countries of North America (Canada, Mexico and the USA) which has evolved into the present-day North America Free Trade Agreement (NAFTA). As it happens, these two groups would also be defined as "regions" when the third, forthcoming guideline is adopted as the basis for classification.

(iii) By this criterion we refer to <u>geographical</u> proximity. Sets of countries relatively close to each other would be defined as a "region". This indeed has guided us in classifying four groups of countries as "regions".

The world (or, rather, most of it) is classified into four "regions" (or, in the terminology used here, "blocs"):

(i) "Free-market Europe" (as it was during the latter half of the 20th century — that is, excluding the formerly planned economies of the Soviet bloc);

(ii) North America;

(iii)   South America; and

(iv)   "East Asia" — which stands, for brevity, for East and Southeast Asia and Oceania.[1]

All of the four are "geographical" regions, in the sense of containing countries which are geographically reasonably close to each other. Two of the regions — "South America" and "East Asia" — are predominantly just that (though South America does have several preferential agreements of some significance within it). The other two, Europe (in particular) and North America, have also adopted strong policies of regional integration.

Before turning to the main issue of our exploration we wish to suggest an indication as to whether our classification of "regions" may make some sense, beyond the arbitrary manner in which we have made our classification. To have some meaning, membership in a "region" should imply some bias of a member country in favor of trade with its partners to the region. An indication of bias (whatever its source) which we shall employ, to test its existence, is the "intensity ratio" in trade among countries (see definition and use in Chapter 2). We recall that a ratio of unity implies "neutrality" of these trade flows, a ratio above unity the existence of favorable bias, and a ratio below unity its obverse.

We have estimated the intensity ratios in trade flows between each pair of countries in each given region.[2] Presenting here all those ratios

---

[1] Left out of the analysis are primarily the following areas: (i) The Indian Sub-Continent, (ii) West Asia, (iii) The African Continent, and (iv) the formerly Soviet bloc. Exclusion of Africa originates from the presumption that there is not much sense in exploring "regionalism" within this continent. Exclusion of the Soviet bloc is due to a variety of reasons, including scarcity and unreliability of data over much of the period, differences in definitions, and the fact that much of what became "international" trade within this group of countries in the 1990s was formerly "domestic" trade within the Soviet Union. We have also left out of our classification potential "regions" which are of small size, in terms of their aggregates of trade and potential trade relations among them. Main examples are the countries of Central America and the Caribbean, and the Arab countries of the Middle East (in both instances, despite the geographic proximity being supplemented by cultural affinity). In both instances, economic structures of the relevant participants would suggest, a-priori, only minor trade flows among them. Altogether, the four blocs analyzed here contributed close to 75% of world exports in 1962 and around 80% in 2010. In most of the following discussion, the term "world" will stand, for brevity, for the aggregate of the four blocs, rather than the actual world as a whole.

[2] As in many other instances, we have confined the exploration to exports. That is, the intensity ratio of a country's trade with its partner is the share of the ("home") country's

(several hundreds) would be cumbersome and probably not instructive. Instead, we have taken the <u>median</u> of a given country's trade ratios with the individual country members of the region to represent the country's intensity ratio in trade with the "region". The outcome of these estimates is presented, by regions and individual countries, in Table 8.1.

The outcome appears to be rather clear-cut. In all four blocs we have termed as "regions", trade (exports) of member countries are

Table 8.1: Intensity ratios in regional trade

Region and Country	Ratio	Region and Country	Ratio
Free-Market Europe		Brazil	5.33
Austria	0.99	Chile	4.37
Denmark	1.42	Colombia	1.53
Finland	0.98	Ecuador	1.53
Germany	1.89	Paraguay	17.04
Ireland	0.94	Peru	16.8
Italy	1.24	Uruguay	4.97
Netherlands	1.82	**Median**	**4.97**
Norway	1.63	*East Asia*	
Portugal	1.29	Australia	2.10
Spain	1.07	Cambodia	0.33
Sweden	1.21	China	1.55
Switzerland	0.98	Hong Kong	0.90
UK	1.80	Indonesia	2.40
Median	**1.29**	Japan	1.90
North America		Korea (Rep.)	1.59
Canada	3.19	Malaysia	2.81
Mexico	3.76	New Zealand	1.29
USA	6.97	Singapore	2.99
Median	**3.76**	Thailand	2.30
South America		Viet Nam	1.52
Argentina	12.59	**Median**	**1.90**
Belize	0.01	**Overall Median**	**1.63**

<u>exports</u> to the partner in the country's aggregate exports, relative to the partner's share in aggregate world <u>imports</u>.

definitely biased towards intra-regional trade flows. Of an aggregate of 38 countries presented in the table, the intensity ratio falls below unity in only seven; in five of these the ratio is in fact in the proximity of unity (the remaining two instances are Cambodia and Brazil). By this yardstick, thus, all the blocs we have designated as "regions" indeed qualify to be so termed. Perhaps surprisingly, the region which displays the least bias towards intra-regional trade is Europe. In this region, the median intra-regional intensity ratio is 1.29 — obviously above unity, but not by much. In four instances out of the fourteen participants, the ratio is <u>below</u> unity (a rare instance in the other regions), though in all four the ratio is very close to unity. On the other extreme stands — again, perhaps unexpectedly — the region of Latin America, in which the median ratio for the region is as high as 4.37, and all individual ratios except one (for Belize) are much above unity. In a less extreme, but still obvious manner, the region of <u>East Asia</u> also appears to demonstrate a strong bias towards intra-regional trade. The median ratio for the region is above two, and all individual ratios (with the exception of Cambodia) are clearly above unity. Finally, perhaps least surprisingly, a strong bias towards intra-regional trade is displayed by the outcome for <u>North America</u>. In terms of <u>number</u> of countries (<u>not</u> weight of trade) it is a very small region, with just three members, but among these three trade is biased towards intra-group trade perhaps more strongly than within any other association of a similar size. To sum up: By the yardstick of intensity of intra-bloc trade flows all these four blocs may indeed be reasonably classified as "regions", with the surprising weakness of Europe.

We may now proceed with the exploration of the main issue of this research, namely, the role of regional trade in the overall development of global trade.[3]

---

[3] In probably the most comprehensive empirical analysis of regionalism in trade at the time, Thorbecke (1960) added to it another measure, namely, the extent of multilateral vs bilateral trade in trade flows within the region and in trade of the region's members with third countries, with a presumption that multilateral exchange should be more common in intra-regional trade. We shall refer to this aspect in a separate Annex, at the end of this chapter.

Table 8.2: Share of intra-regional trade in world trade (Exports of Goods)

	Share of Intra-Bloc Trade in Bloc's Aggregate (1)	Share of Bloc's Aggregate in World Trade (2)	Size Adjusted index of Intra-Bloc Trade (=(1)/(2)) (3)
	a. 1962		
Free-Market Europe	0.34	0.35	1.02
North America	0.31	0.26	1.18
South America	0.08	0.06	1.21
East Asia	0.25	0.08	3.13
	b. 2010		
Free-Market Europe	0.58	0.32	1.80
North America	0.49	0.14	3.60
South America	0.20	0.04	5.50
East Asia	0.50	0.31	1.61

Share of aggregate (4-blocs) intra-bloc trade in world aggregate

1962 = 0.29, 2010 = 0.51.

The Size and Development of Regional Trading

The measure adopted here to indicate the performance of regional trading is the one commonly applied in empirical studies of this issue: the share of intra-regional trade (exports) in the region's aggregate trade. This measure is presented in Table 8.2

Country Definition of "Blocs"

The first two columns of Table 8.2 require no explanation, but the third, column (3), does. The measure represented here (one, perhaps, of several alternatives) is intended to address the impact of the <u>size</u> of a bloc on the apparent degree of intra-bloc trade. Intuitively it seems clear that the larger the size of a group of countries, the higher the share of trade carried within the group should be. Taken to the extreme, suppose the group includes, within it, countries which provide 99% of world trade. Practically all trade

a. Free-Market Europe	Austria; Belgium; Denmark; Finland; France; Germany; Greece; Ireland; Italy; Luxembourg; Netherland; Norway; Portugal; Spain; Sweden; Switzerland; UK
b. North America	Canada; Mexico; USA
c. South America	Argentina; Belize; Bolivia; Brazil; Chile; Colombia; Ecuador; Paraguay; Peru; Uruguay; Venezuela
d. "East Asia" (referring to East and Southeast Asia and Oceania)	Australia; Cambodia; China; Hong Kong; Indonesia; Japan; Korea Rep; Laos; Malaysia; New Zealand; Philippines; Singapore; Taiwan; Thailand; Vietnam

of the group's members would then be conducted within the group, and the share of intragroup trade in the group's aggregate trade would approach unity. This represents a fact, but it provides no indication of the tendency of the group's members to trade with each other rather than with outsiders. Hence, to abstract from the impact of sheer size on the share of intra-bloc trade in its aggregate, column (1) is divided by the bloc's share in world trade, recorded in column (2), to yield the measure represented in column (3). Notice that this measure is no longer a share, or a proportion, of one magnitude in another. It is, in a way, an index number, which may potentially (and often does) exceed unity. By itself, it provides no meaning; it acquires significance only in comparisons over areas or over time.[4]

We turn, now, to the findings presented in Table 8.2. Several inferences suggest themselves.

(i)   First, observing the aggregate intra-bloc shares presented at the bottom of the table, a remarkable increase of this manifestation of

---

[4] This index cannot be decomposed except for the two components of which it is originally made. Specifically, consider the following issue. The extent of the share of intra-regional trade, in any given "region", is a function of two elements. One is the "true" element of regional inclination, namely, the tendency of the region's members to trade with each other. The other is, as noted, the aggregate size of the "region". The index devised here cannot, unfortunately, separate these two elements. This issue also served the basis for our earlier analysis of defining a region through the use of intensity ratios.

"regionalism" appears to have taken place; the share of this trade in aggregate world trade (the universe of the four blocs) increased from close to 30% in 1962 to over 50% in 2010. Thus, the remarkable expansion of world trade over this period (not shown in the table) has taken place, to a large extent, through a particular expansion of regional trade. A word of caution, though; it is conceivable that this apparent outcome represents, to one degree or another, not a true increase of regional trade but a shift from the division of the world from one class of "regions" to another. We shall return soon to this issue.

(ii) Special attention should be paid to Europe, in which the share of intra-bloc trade in the bloc's aggregate rose markedly — from 0.34 in 1962 to 0.58 in 2010 — though this does not exceed dramatically the change in the aggregate of the three other blocs. The expansion of intra-regional trade in Europe is not explained by an increased share of Europe in the world's aggregate trade: the latter remained on roughly the same level, of about one third with a rather slight fall, between the starting and ending points of the period. Thus, the adjusted share of intra-bloc trade (column (3)) increased, over the period, to practically the same extent as the simple share of intra-bloc trade. Due to both its size and its high share of intra-bloc trade, Europe provided roughly one half of the world's aggregate intra-regional trade in both 1962 and 2010.

Europe (including the UK) has always, in the modern era, been predominant in world trade. At the middle of the 20th century — about the starting point of the period surveyed here — roughly two thirds of global flows consisted of an exchange in which at least one of the two partners was a European country.[5] But Europe has developed into a "region" only in recent decades. As it emerged from WWII (and even more so prior to it), major European trading countries were centers of "regions" of their own, in which non-European economies served as a periphery. The region in which the UK was central, the "Sterling Area", or "the Area of Imperial Preferences", was most notable. But other European countries — such as France, the Netherlands, Belgium, Spain, or Portugal — followed similar patterns. The essence of each such region was the trade of each "center"

---

[5] Consult Michaely (1968), with additional references provided in this source.

with its (present or recent past) colonies — more predominant for the colonies, but also of major importance for the center.[6]

This brings us to the point raised earlier, namely: the examination of intraregional trade in a set of four "blocs" within the "four blocs" as it is carried out here, overlooks the drastic decline of several "regions" as they had existed at the middle of the 20th century, particularly the Sterling Area. Within the present analysis, we can only venture the presumption that "new" regions only partly replaced the "old" ones, whereas in part, they represent a "new" expansion of regionalism in world trade.[7]

The role of the UK keeps appearing in the discussion of regionalism in Europe. From being the center of its separate "region", over the last half-century, the UK became an integral member of the region of Europe. This change in the geographic pattern of the UK's trade has been associated with a radical change in the commodity structure of the country's trade, with

[6]We address here the share of colonial trading in the trade of the <u>metropolitan</u> countries, not in the trade of the colonies. But to give an impression of the latter role, which was much heavier, we cite here findings in E. Kleiman (1976) (Table 1).
<u>Share of Metropolitan Country in the Trade of its Dependencies 1960-7</u> (in percent of dependency's trade)

Metropolitan Country	Exports	Imports
UK	39.6	35.2
France	58.7	66.2
Portugal	32.0	36.7
Belgium	45.5	25.8
Italy	54.4	31.6

[7]E. Thorbecke (1960, Table 48, p. 37) provides the following estimates.
<u>Sterling Area Exports, 1956 (in per cent)</u>

Intra-area trade/total area trade	46.5
Intra-area trade/aggregate world trade	10.9
Total area trade/aggregate world trade	23.5

Thus, the intra-regional trade within the Sterling Area accounted, at the middle of the twentieth century, for about 11 per cent of the world's aggregate trade. This may be compared with the aggregate (Table 8-2) of intra-bloc trade in the four blocs' total of 29 percent in 1962 and 51 percent in 2010. The other "regions" with European "centers" were quantitatively of much less significance.

causality probably running both ways. The UK's trade prior to the 1960s could be largely characterized as the exchange of its industrial goods for the imports of primary goods. This pattern, it should be noted, was distinctly different from that of the other major European industrial countries, whose trade even then — and definitely now — consisted mostly of the exchange of manufacturers for other manufactures. By the end of the period surveyed, this became mostly also the commodity trade pattern of the UK.

(iii)   The bloc of North America provides another interesting observation. As seen from column (1) in Table 8.2, the share of intra-bloc in the bloc's aggregate trade increased markedly between 1962 and 2010 — by almost 60%. This is quite close to this share's increase in Europe, over the period. But the relative expansion of intra-bloc trade is more remarkable, in the case of North America, in view of the fact that this bloc's aggregate trade contracted as a proportion of world trade. This proportion fell by almost half over the period, from 0.26 to 0.14. Thus, the adjusted share of intra-bloc trade (column (3)) about tripled, increasing from 1.18 to 3.60. In this sense, the intensity of intra-bloc trade increased in North America much more than it did in Europe. Much of this may have originated from the conclusion of NAFTA — though, again, with the limited capacity of the analytical context used here, this must remain a matter of supposition.

This performance has been shared and even exceeded by the bloc of South America. Here, the share of intra-bloc in the bloc's aggregate trade increased, over the period, by as much as 150%, from 0.08 to 0.20. Given that the relative size of this bloc's trade is not just small but has further declined, over the period — from 6% to 4% of the worlds' aggregate — the increase of the adjusted index was even more dramatic, rising from 1.21 to 5.50. Due to the small relative size of the bloc, though, the impact of this impressive change on the tendency of global trade toward regionalization was necessarily small; the share of the bloc's intra-bloc trade in the aggregate (four blocs) intra-bloc trade amounted to only 3% in 2010.

(iv)   Finally, the large bloc of "Asia" provides contrasting observations. The share of intra-bloc trade in the bloc's aggregate increased markedly over the period; it doubled, from 0.25 in 1962 to 0.50 in 2010. In the latter year, this trade provided close to 40% of the world's aggregate intra-bloc trade. In that sense, this region became almost as important as Europe, whereas it was merely one-fifth of Europe in 1962. But this performance must have been predominantly due to the relative expansion of this bloc's trade in the world's aggregate; over the period surveyed, the share of the bloc increased about four-fold. Thus, the adjusted index of intra-bloc trade actually fell over the period by as much as a half — from 3.13 in 1962 to 1.62 in 2010. In fact, this is the only bloc (of the four) in which the adjusted index fell rather than increased. It may be presumed, thus, that in the case of Asia the apparent impressive expansion of intra-bloc trade simply reflects the dramatic expansion of the bloc's trade rather than a genuine increase in the tendency of the bloc's members to trade with each other.[8]

As has been pointed out all along, the quantitative analysis of the extent of regionalism in trade suggested here is tentative, and its inferences must be hedged. The analysis may be improved, or supplemented, in a variety of ways, some of which have been indicated in the text or in its footnotes. Nevertheless, the evidence presented here does support a conclusion that global trade patterns have changed, over the last half-century in the direction of further intensifying the extent of regionalism in world trade. Thus, while there has been a very impressive intensification of globalization, in the sense of increased relative importance of world trade, the term "globalization" should be qualified: much of this trade expansion has taken place not within the context of the "globe" as a whole, but rather via the channel of trade within specific regions.

Annex 8.1: Multilateral Balancing in Regional Trade

The Issue

Is there a tendency, or a bias, towards a high degree of multilateral balancing of trade <u>within</u> regional trading blocs rather than in trade of bloc members with outsiders? Such bias is indicated persistently in the aforementioned, basic study by Thorbecke on regionalism in the first half of the 20th

---

[8] "Presumed" because, as noted earlier, the analytical tools employed here do not allow the separation of impacts of these two potential origins of regional trading.

century. We shall ask here, first, what is the <u>meaning</u> of such bias; then, whether there are <u>a-priori</u> reasons to expect such a bias; and last, whether some reasonable measure, (or measures), may be suggested to estimate the actual existence of a bias (or its absence).

The extent of multilateral balancing in a country's trade is the <u>relative</u> size of such balancing, "relative" being heavily emphasized. That is, a high degree of multilateral balancing is defined not as a large <u>size</u> of such balancing but rather as its <u>ratio</u> to the country's aggregate trade (or, which is basically equivalent, to the size of the country's bilateral trading). This appears to be an emphasis of a trivially understood element, but it is nevertheless important to keep this element in mind.

A rather intuitive response would be that, indeed, the bias at hand should <u>a-priori</u> be expected. When a country tends (presumably) to conduct its bilateral trade with the region's members more intensively than with others, so should its multilateral transactions with the region's members be expected to be. But here comes the element we have just emphasized, namely, the magnitude looked for is not the aggregate <u>size</u> of the country's multilateral trade, but rather its proportion in the country's own aggregate trade or, to make it more visible, the ratio of multilaterally-cleared trade to the size of the country's <u>bilateral</u> trade with the region's members. And the latter is expected, to start with, to be particularly intensive. There is thus no presumption, without other pieces of evidence or reasoning, to expect the <u>ratio</u> of multilateral to bilateral trade to be higher (or lower) in the country's trade with the region's members than in its trade with the outside world.

Empirical Estimation

To measure the element of multilateral balancing we use the following index:[9]

1. *Index of country's multilateral balancing of trade*

$$I = \frac{\Sigma \left| X_{ki} - M_{ki} \right|}{X_{\cdot j}} \Big/ 2$$

---

[9]This is a somewhat simplified version of the index formulated in Michaely (1962).

where,

X_{ki} = export of country j ("home") to country k (partner)

M_{ki} = imports of country j from country k; and

X_j = Aggregate exports of country j.[10]

This index ranges from zero, a completely bilateral trade of (in each of the trade flows of country $X_{kj} - M_{kj} = 0$, hence the level of the index is zero) to unity, where in each trade flows, with a partner, $X_{kj} - M_{kj} = X_{ki} = 1$ and the index becomes unity.

To address the issue at hand, we devise two sub-indexes of multilateralism: one for each country's trade with partners to its region; and the other for its trade, with the rest of the world (ROW).

Take countries one to *n* as the universe — the world. Of these, countries *f* to *k*, including country *j*, constitute a "region", whereas all other countries, *l* to *n*, are the rest of the world (ROW). We define now subindices of multilateral balancing for country *j*, one for its trade within the region and another for its trade with ROW.

2. *The index of multilateral balancing within region*

$$I_r \sum_{l-k} \frac{|X_{kj} - M_{kj}|}{X_j} \bigg/ 2, \text{ where country k is a regional partner.}$$

3. *The index of multilateral balancing of a regional member in trade with ROW*

$$I_w \sum_{k-n} \frac{|X_{nj} - M_{nj}|}{X_j} \bigg/ 2, \text{ where n is a non-regional partner.}$$

The estimates of these two indices will be presented shortly in Annex 8.1. But first, let us issue two <u>denials</u>. That is, it should be indicated for what purposes the estimate at hand should <u>not</u> be used.

---

[10]This formulation assumes implicitly that country j's aggregate trade is balanced (a valid assumption, in a rough way, for almost all present-day countries), hence, that X_j stands also for M_j.

First, the estimate should <u>not</u> be used for comparison over <u>space</u>; specifically, for comparing regional members with members of other regions. The reason for the invalidity of such potential comparisons is the crucial impact of <u>size</u>. As has been noted in the text in a similar context, the larger a region, the more intensive should be multilateral balancing within it. To make an extreme example, when the "region" consists of the overwhelming majority of the world (in terms of trade flows), practically all multilateral balancing will take place within the region, and very little beyond it. Comparisons of regions of varying sizes may thus be misleading when the <u>tendency</u> to conduct multilateral balancing (i.e., a <u>bias</u> towards these trade flows) is addressed.

Similarly, a comparison over time of the extent of multilateral balancing within a given region would be distorted when, as may often be expected, the size of the region (once more in terms of trade flows) changes over time.

It is conceivable that the indices we are using might be reformulated in order to accommodate this impact of size, but since these comparisons over space and time are <u>not</u> our main concern, we have not explored the possibility of such reformulation and find it suffice to indicate, as we have just done, the potential flaws in such comparisons.

We shall now turn to our main concern, namely, the exploration of the extent to which, at any <u>given</u> time and for any <u>given</u> region, regional members tend to practice multilateral balancing within the region more (or less) than they practice it in their trade with the rest of the world. This we do by means of the estimates presented in Annex Table 8.2. Column (1) of the table records the estimate yielded by the definition presented earlier; namely, the extent of multilateral balancing <u>within</u> the region i (Column 2), similarly, records the estimates yielded by definition of the extent of multilateral balancing practiced by a region's member in its trade with <u>other</u> countries — the rest of the world. Finally, Column (3) records the ratio of the first measure to the second i yielding thus a measurement of the <u>bias</u> towards multilateral balancing in regional trade. A ratio of unity would indicate <u>no bias</u>: multilateral balancing is practiced within the region with the same intensity as in the trade of regional members with the rest of the world (ROW). A ratio above unity would indicate a bias towards multilateral balancing within the region, whereas a ratio below

Table A.8.1: Multilateral balancing in regional trade
(Indexes of Multilateral Balancing in Trade of)

Region and Country	Regional Members with Regional Partners (1)	Regional Members with ROW (2)	Ratio (1)/(2) (3)
Free-Market Europe			
Austria	0.207	0.248	0.835
Belgium	0.205	0.252	0.814
Denmark	0.270	0.296	0.912
Finland	0.315	0.361	0.873
France	0.224	0.295	0.759
Germany	0.184	0.236	0.780
Ireland	0.283	0.293	0.966
Italy	0.242	0.315	0.768
Netherlands	0.196	0.263	0.745
Norway	0.295	0.326	0.911
Portugal	0.355	0.405	0.877
Spain	0.271	0.395	0.686
Sweden	0.265	0.289	0.917
Switzerland	0.248	0.252	0.984
UK	0.306	0.351	0.872
Median	0.248	0.295	0.872
North America			
Canada	0.187	0.274	0.688
Mexico	0.224	0.337	0.665
USA	0.278	0.433	0.642
Median	0.224	0.337	0.665
South America			
Argentina	0.271	0.364	0.745
Brazil	0.261	0.388	0.673
Chile	0.687	0.438	1.669
Colombia	0.471	0.455	1.035
Ecuador	0.430	0.479	0.898

Table A.8.1: *(Continued)*

Region and Country	Regional Members with Regional Partners (1)	Regional Members with ROW (2)	Ratio (1)/(2) (3)
Peru	0.658	0.449	1.460
Median	0.471	0.438	1.035
East Asia			
Australia	0.451	0.427	1.056
China	0.369	0.360	1.025
Hong Kong	0.235	0.261	0.900
Indonesia	0.394	0.403	0.978
Japan	0.367	0.393	0.934
Malaysia	0.259	0.295	0.878
New Zealand	0.425	0.424	0.979
Singapore	0.229	0.288	0.795
Viet Nam	0.591	0.496	1.192
Thailand	0.323	0.365	0.885
Median	0.369	0.365	0.978
Overall Median	0.271	0.351	0.877

unity would indicate the opposite — a more intense multilateral balancing in trade with the ROW than in trade within the region. The table is arranged by regions, as defined in the main text of the chapter.

The findings recorded in Annex Table 8.1 indicate that, by and large, no bias is suggested towards multilateral balancing in regional trade or against it. The ratios presented in Column (3) tend to congregate in the proximity of unity; and, with the exception of the trade of members of the region of South America, with not much variance around the value of unity.

A notable exception is that of the region of North America. It is a small one in terms of number of members, consisting of just three countries. The ratio at hand is substantially and consistently below unity, in the range of 0.642 to 0.688. This is indeed a unique region: among the 33 other countries listed in Annex Table 8.1 only two — Brazil and

Spain — record ratios as low as those of the three North American countries. It consists of one major trader, the US, and two much smaller partners, Canada and Mexico. In each of the trade flows of the two other partners with the US, this trade is predominant. Relatively little trade is conducted between the two minor partners; thus, not much room is left for offsetting imbalances in trade flows with the US by multilateral balancing within the region.

Thus, our overall conclusion is that the hypothesis of practicing extensively multilateral balancing in regional trade is <u>not</u> borne out; nor is its opposite, with the exception of the region of North America. By and large, membership in trade regions does not appear to be conductive to either intensive multilateral balancing or to be its opposite.

This outcome of the empirical analysis should not be surprising in view of our earlier <u>a-priori</u> analysis, which pointed out the absence of universal grounds for a special encouragement of multilateral balancing within regions. Not just "natural" circumstances, but even the existence of preferential trade agreements should <u>not</u> lead to a biased outcome. In a world in which less than universal currency convertibility is practiced, a preferential currency region (i.e., a higher level of currency convertibly within a region than outside it) <u>should</u> indeed promote multilateral balancing in a region's trade. This was a correct description of the world in a large part of the 20th century, up to the 1970s. On the other hand, in the world of today, it is not a relevant factor.

Chapter 9

Focus on Europe

Europe's Dominant Role in Trade[1]

Europe is the hub of world trade. In an earlier year of the period investigated in this study, 1970, the proportion of the combined size of Europe's exports and imports in its world equivalence was 52.1 percent — that is, over half of the trade. This proportion has declined over the period, but it still amounted in 2010 to 32.9 percent — that is, about a third.

This dominance could <u>not</u> be explained by Europe's size. In terms of population, Europe's amounted in 2010 to about 5.5 percent of the world's aggregate. Put differently the size of trade per capita was in that year roughly ten times as high in Europe than in the world at large. Since Europe is evidently a rich region, a more relevant measure should represent size by income, rather than population. Here, too, the difference still exists. The ratio of exports to income in Europe (in 2010) is 28.8 percent, versus 22.7 percent for the world as a whole.

Having stated that, we should still note the decline of this status over the last two generations. The two ratios just recorded for Europe's share in world trade — 52.1 percent in 1970 and 32.9 percent in 2010 — show this decline in an obvious manner. This, it should be noted, is <u>not</u> related to any after-effects of WWII, since 1970 may certainly be looked at as an already "normal" year. This declining share of Europe also appears in the

---

[1] "Europe" is defined here, as in most of our analysis, as the aggregate of European countries which were defined as "free-market" economies over most of the period.

157

more elaborate analysis carried out in Chapter 2, where the progress of the foreign trade ratio (FTR) is recorded. It is shown there that Europe's FTR doubled from 1960 to 2010. This is much below the increasing-share performance of the USA — in which the FTR about quadrupled — and somewhat below the rate of change in the rest of the world (i.e., excluding Europe and the USA). The formal analysis carried out in that chapter indicates a trend of "conversion" of FTRs — a tendency to increase <u>less</u> over the period the <u>higher</u> the initial FTR. But, given the large role played by Europe's members in determining trade patterns, it does not follow necessarily that patterns "conform" to the rule; they may rather be setting it.

To sum up: Europe's trade continues to be particularly large, both in its share in world trade and as a proportion of its general economic activity. But its outstanding position, on both scores, has become less prominent over the last half century.

Finally, it should be noted that our exploration of <u>multilateral balancing</u> in trade (Chapter 8) has shown that in this aspect of the geographic pattern of trade flows, Europe, despite its dominant role and unique features, does <u>not</u> differ from other regions of the world in two aspects. First, in its aggregate trade flows, it exhibits a similar relative intensity of multilateral balancing as is common for the average country in the ROW. Second — and more meaningful in the present context — Europe's trade does not exhibit a trend of multilateral balancing <u>within</u> the region which is, on the whole, very different from the extent of such balancing in Europe's trade with the rest of the world.

We move now to an important element of Europe's trade: the significance of intra-European trade. We noticed earlier (Chapter 8) that the component of intra-regional trade is more important in Europe than in other regional blocs in the world. We shall now reproduce some of the earlier discussion and expand on it.

Table 9.1 presents the basic data. Columns (1) and (2) are self-explanatory. In Column (3) the ratio of the second to the first column — the ratio of intra-European to Europe's aggregate trade — is recorded. It may be seen that this ratio remained almost unchanged over the period surveyed; a look back at the findings of Chapter 5 will demonstrate that this ratio is particularly high. Thus, much of Europe's dominant share in world trade may be explained by trade <u>within</u> this region.

Table 9.1: Intra-European trade vs. trade with the ROW

	Europe's Aggregate Trade (X+n) (1)	Intra-European Trade (2)	Share of Intra-European Trade (=(2)/(1)) (3)	Trade with ROW (4)	Europe's GDP (5)	Ratio[2] of Trade with ROW to GDP $\left(= \frac{(4)/(5)}{2}\right)$ (6)
1970	488	188	0.39	300	834	18.0
2010	15,246	5,586	0.37	9,600	16,666	28.8

This leads us to an issue which is sometimes raised in an extremely hypothetical manner. Suppose Europe is not a multitude of political identities but one political unit like, say, the United States. Its intra-regional trade thus becomes a domestic rather than an international trade. Under this hypothetical regime, what would Europe's international trade look like? Columns (4) to (6) of Table 9.1 are addressed to this issue.

Column (4), which is the difference between Europe's aggregate trade and its intra-trade flows, records the trade of Europe with the ROW, that is, the international trade of "Europe" (the "single state" in this exercise). This trade, we recall, is somewhat over 60 percent of the overall trade of Europe as a multi-state entity. In Column (5) Europe's GDP is recorded; and Column (6) presents Europe's international trade, as defined here, as a ratio to its GDP (note the explanation at the bottom of the table of the nature of this estimate).

The last ratio appears to be about 18 percent at the start of the period, 1970, and 29 percent at its close, 2010. Whether trade ratios are "high" or "low" may be judged by two relevant comparisons. First, a look over time; the ratio at hand presumably increased over the period. The (fictitious) "United States of Europe" thus appears to have increased substantially its place in world trade. Second, a comparison with other entities. Needless to say, it would be impossible to find an entity with an identity equivalent to that of "Europe", but two political units which might come close come to mind: the USA and China. In terms of aggregate income (and even of

---

[2]The "normal" ratio required here would be that of exports to GDP. But since "Intra-European" trade (hence trade with ROW) cannot (conceptually) be separated into "exports" and "imports", we replace "exports" by aggregate trade divided by two.

size of territory, though obviously not in size of population), these may be regarded as being in the same league with "Europe". The ratio of exports to GDP in 2010 appears to be 12.4 percent in the USA, and 26.3 percent in China. Thus, "Europe" is as much a global trader, in this sense, as China; and much more than the USA. In both the USA and China, the ratios of trade to income (not shown here) increased over the period substantially more than in "Europe". The latter's position as a global trader has thus declined over the period, but remained strong even at its end.

Europe's Basic Trade Structure

As is evident, and has just been recorded, Europe is a high-income region, its per-capita income being several times higher than the average for the rest of the world. High income and specialization in highly processed goods being closely related, Europe should naturally be expected to have a trade structure which reflects this pattern of specialization. This is a well-known phenomenon. It is recorded in Table 9.2 by means of presenting the shares of manufactures in both exports and imports, and for both a start year (1965) and the end of the period under analysis (2010). The shares are recorded for each individual European country (including most regional members), as well as (through an <u>unweighted</u> average) for the region as a whole.

It seems, first, that the share of manufacturing is indeed high. In the start year, 1965, it is over one half for 10 out of the 15 countries presented; for Europe as a whole, it is 55 percent. Even without a formal analysis, it seems clear that the share of manufacturing is related (positively) to income; the higher-income members of the region exhibit a higher share of manufacturing in their exports. By the end of the period, 2010, this share changed only by a little, in most individual countries and in the region as a whole. In about half the countries the share has (slightly) declined, while increasing (again slightly) for the rest. For the aggregate of countries, the share declined imperceptibly. Not surprisingly, the share has increased markedly in two countries, Greece and Spain, which were relatively poor at the start of the period.

In view of our earlier findings (Chapter 3), it is not surprising to see that the structure of <u>imports</u> is not, as a rule, much different from that of exports. In 1965, the average share of manufacturing in imports was for the whole region 0.53 percent versus 55 percent for exports. In 2010, the equivalent

Table 9.2: Shares of manufacturing

	1965			**2010**		
	X	**M**	**X-M**	**X**	**M**	**X-M**
	(1)	**(2)**	**(3)**	**(4)**	**(5)**	**(6)**
Austria	0.75	0.60	0.15	0.71	0.63	0.08
Belgium-Lux	0.75	0.54	0.21	0.48	0.48	0
Denmark	0.38	0.58	0.20	0.50	0.63	0.13
Finland	0.57	0.60	0.03	0.70	0.51	0.19
France	0.63	0.44	0.19	0.62	0.61	0.01
Germany	0.72	0.40	0.32	0.69	0.58	0.11
Greece	0.12	0.57	0.45	0.35	0.46	0.11
Ireland	0.24	0.51	0.27	0.26	0.48	0.22
Italy	0.70	0.33	0.37	0.72	0.53	0.19
Netherlands	0.47	0.37	0.10	0.43	0.47	0.03
Norway	0.52	0.65	0.13	0.21	0.68	0.47
Spain	0.33	0.49	0.16	0.60	0.53	0.07
Sweden	0.62	0.63	0.01	0.65	0.60	0.05
Switzerland	0.73	0.60	0.12	0.53	0.62	0.09
UK	0.74	0.34	0.40	0.53	0.58	0.03
Total Europe	0.55	0.53	0.20	0.53	0.56	0.11

shares were again almost identical, but the slight difference changed <u>sign</u>; the average ratio became 56 percent for imports, versus 53 percent for exports. But it is interesting to see that in <u>individual</u> countries, the differences between shares of imports and exports declined materially from the start to the end of the period. This is shown in columns (3) and (6) of Table 9.2, which record the (<u>absolute</u>) differences between the export and import shares. These are mostly lower in 2010 than in 1965. This is true for twelve out of the fifteen countries represented in the table. The mean of the differences in individual countries was 0.21 in 1965, and it fell by close to a half, at 0.12, in the end year 2010. Similarly, the <u>median</u> level decreased between two years from 0.19 to 0.09. These measures are, indeed, low enough for the end of the period, 2010, as to be able to state that, by the gross classification of manufactures vs. primary good, the commodity structures are roughly equal for exports and imports. As noted on an earlier occasion (Chapter 3) the

Table 9.3: Coefficient of commodity concentration in Europe and ROW

	Exports		Imports	
	Mean	**Median**	**Mean**	**Median**
Europe				
1965	24.0	19.3	15.4	15.4
2010	20.7	15.4	14.8	14.2
ROW				
1965	51.0	48.7	21.3	18.5
2010	39.5	32.6	20.1	18.4

dissimilarity of structure in the earlier period was in fact unique to the U.K., in which the most dramatic decline of dissimilarity took place over the period.

Closely related to these developments of trade structure is the exploration of the extent of commodity concentration of trade (see Chapter 4). Table 9.3, derived from the data of that chapter, presents in a summarized way the performance of the beginning and end of the period surveyed. Two observations may be noted.

(1) From the start (1965) to the end (2010) of the period, the level of commodity concentration in European countries declined, but this decline was even much stronger in the ROW. In a sense, this apparently weaker progress in Europe was almost inevitable; the level of concentration was low enough (relative to its level in the ROW) that it left little room for further decline.

(2) At the start of the period, the level of concentration was still significantly lower in Europe's export trade than in its imports, even though the difference between the two was much higher in the ROW. By the period's end, the level of concentration of the two trade flows became much closer; judging by the median, the two levels became almost identical. This is another representation of the tendency, noted earlier, of Europe's rough commodity structures to become quite similar in Europe's exports and imports.[3]

---

[3] One exception originates from the experience of Norway. The vast finding and exploration of oil and gas in this country have led to a drastic increase in the share of these goods in

Europe and Its Colonies: The Fading Trade

A complementary of the increased share of Intra-European trade in Europe's aggregate is, of course, a decline of the shares of other geographical components in Europe's aggregate trade. Of particular interest is the role played by Europe's trade with its (former) colonies,[4] which in the past had been regarded as a mainstay of Europe's trade and even a main factor of geo-political concerns. This element of trade will be addressed in the present section.

Table 9.4 records Europe's trade with its colonies. It appears from these findings that the trade flow of the former to the latter are at minimal level: roughly, in the neighborhood of 4 percent or slightly above, compare this level, for instance, with intra-European trade flows — shown earlier in Columns (1) and (2) of Table 9.1 — to be about 37 percent.

This is true for both the earlier post-war year of 1970 as well as for the period's end year of 2010. Thus, Europe's trade with its former colonies appears to now be of almost no significance.[5]

Table 9.4: Share of (former) colonies in Europe's trade (in b. dollars and percent)

	Aggregate Trade of Europe (1)	Trade of Europe with Colonies (2)	Share of Trade with Colonies (=(2)/(1)) (3)
1970	299	13	4.5
2010	9.660	398	4.1

Norway's exports and hence to a dramatic increase in the share of primary goods and the relative decline of manufactured exports. Excluding Norway, the average share of manufacture exports of Europe as a whole has remained stable, changing over the period from 55 to just 56 percent.

[4] We use here the term "colonies" for any form of political dependence of a territorial entity on a metropolitan country. The legal terms of this dependence would obviously differ from one case to another.

[5] The topic of the present analysis is the significance of Europe's trade with the colonies for Europe and not for the colonies, hence, we do not undertake here an investigation of the latter element. We note briefly the significance of that element by reproducing findings of a study (Kleiman, 1976) which was devoted to this issue. This is done in Table 9.4.

Table 9.5:   Percentage of trade with colonies

	1938	**1953**	**1955**	**2010**
UK				
Exports	14.3	18.2	20.1	5.5
Imports	11.8	15.6	16.9	2.7
Total/2	13.0	16.9	18.5	4.1
France				
Exports	26.9	39.2	31.8	NA
Imports	20.9	26.5	24.9	NA
Total/2	26.9	32.8	28.3	2.1

Source: For 1938-1955: Data in E. Thorbecke (1960),
Table 4, pp. 15–18.

This is quite a different phenomenon than the attention these trade flows attracted in the years prior to World War II. We do not have appropriate records for Europe's trade as a whole for that period. Instead, we shall restrict our evidence to the two major European countries involved in colonial trade, the UK and France. The comparison of pre-WWII with the post-war years is carried out in Table 9.5.

It appears, from Table 9.5, that the decline of Europe's trade with the colonies did <u>not</u> take place immediately after WWII. To the contrary, the colonies' shares were even somewhat higher in the mid-1950s than in the pre-war year 1938. This absence of decline was probably due to the time lag involved in any adjustment to changing circumstances, as well as to the fact that in the early post-war years most of the "Colonies" involved

Table 9.4:   Share of trade of colonies with metropolitan country, (in percent)

	Exports (1)	**Imports** (2)	**Average** =(1)/(2) (3)
UK Colonies	46.0	38.9	42.5
French Colonies	52.7	60.5	56.6

Source: E. Kleinman (1976), Table 1.

The proportions recorded here — slightly less than a half for UK Colonies and slightly above it for the Colonies of France — far exceed, of course, the recorded equivalent shares in the trade of Europe with Europe's colonies. It is dramatically higher for the Colonies than for their metropolitan European countries, the latter being of minimal significance.

still maintained their political dependence on the metropolitan countries. Thus, the shares of the Colonies in the trade of the metropolitan countries were still as high as close to one-fifth in the case of the UK and over one-fourth in the case of France. The decline of these shares to a level of almost no significance — just over 4 percent — thus took place between the mid-1950s and the late 1960s.[6] During this period, Europe's trade with its colonies almost vanished. Much of this development is most probably due to changing commodity structures in both Europe and the colonies. It may be suggested that of even more importance was the general liberalization of global trade, which lowered the impact on the size of trade of preferences granted by the existence of political dependence.

The Impact of Distance: The World Without Europe

We have seen, in Chapter 6, that the impact of geographic distance on the size of trade is much lower than the conventional wisdom holds. But, of particular significance to our present discussion, we have also established, as a-priori analysis should also indicate, that this impact, to the extent that it exists, is stronger when relatively short distances are involved and much weaker when partners are relatively far away from each other. Without suggesting here further precise numerical indications we know, first, that Europe provides much of the world's trade, and, second, that intra-European trade, which involves trade among near-by partners, is of much significance both for its shares in European as well as in global trade. Hence, it may be suspected that the general findings about the impact of distance may be heavily dependent on European trade, both with other European countries and with the rest of the world (ROW) which is further away. In this section, we examine the impact of distance in a world which abstracts from the trade of Europe, in this way indicating how important the trade of Europe is for conclusions concerning global trade.

In Chapter 6, we recorded (in Table 6.3) that the distance coefficient of the intensity ratio for the universe of countries is –0.094, which indicates an elasticity of trade to distance of close to –0.1. We repeat now the same

---

[6] It should be noted that in comparing findings in Tables 9.1 and 9.5, we involve in the first instance "Europe" as a whole versus just the UK and France in the latter. But due to the large shares of the UK and France in "Europe" the comparison is meaningful, though the specific numbers should not be understood to give a precise indication.

analysis for the same universe but <u>excluding</u> the countries of Europe. The coefficient now appears to be –0.055 and $R^2 = 0.039$ (as before, it is significant at any desired level. That is, the elasticity in question, low to start with, is lowered by almost a half, and appears to indicate that distance has almost no impact on the size of trade flows among trading partners (e.g., doubling the distance would lower trade by 5 percent). That is, the impact of distance on trade — low as it is due to a major extent to the trade patterns of the countries of Europe.[7]

The finding of a very weak impact of distance on the size of trade conforms with expectations based on the relative size of transportation costs. We have discussed this at some length in Chapter 6, but another point of view may be added. The apparent major discrepancy between this <u>a-priori</u> expectation and the high elasticity of trade flow to distance (mostly around unity) found in much of the conventional literature may be explained by the assumption that "distance" may be a proxy to other variables which should have much impact on trade, such as a common culture, language, religion, history, judicial and political systems or common borders. This may indeed be true. But note that such explanations would apply predominantly to Europe, and not much of it would hold for trade flows among most other countries. The bottom line is that the study of the impact of distance actually amounts, to a major extent, to a study of "the significance of being a European country". Presumably this indirect reference should be complemented by studying <u>directly</u> institutional and historical attributes which would explore the issue of what makes Europe's countries trade in the directions they actually do.

---

[7]The removal of Europe from the universe of observations may potentially introduce some bias into the analysis: Trade flows of European countries with the ROW may — and should — differ from other global trade flows in their level of distance from trading partner. In Chapter 7 (Table 7.1) we have estimated the <u>distance level</u> of each country's trade flows. Examining these levels, we find that the <u>coefficient of variance</u> of the individual observations is 0.654 for the world as a whole; 0.302 for just Europe; and 0.423 for the ROW. The restriction of the observations to the ROW, rather than the world as a whole is thus found to indeed lower the distance of the observations somewhat. Whether, or to what extent, this contributes to the finding of different impacts of distance on the level of trade, in the ROW versus the world as a whole we cannot judge.

Annex A

A Compendium of Indices

In this book, we use a variety of indices to indicate structural attributes of global trade, and their changes over time. A minority of these are measures practiced commonly in the literature. Others are devices formulated by Michaely and presented in earlier publications over the last half century. The rest are measures developed in the present study to investigate its subject matters. We regard it useful to assemble here the indices used, whether old or new. This may help both in reading the present text — in which an index first presented in one chapter may often be used in others, where it would not be fully described again — and in making the indices more readily available to other potential researchers who may find one or another of them to be helpful in their own explorations. The indices are listed here in the order of the chapters in which they first appear.[1]

Notation

j = An individual country of a universe of n countries. When two countries are involved, j is the "home" country; k is the "partner"
i = an individual good or activity
$0, 1$ are start and end years of a period ("base" and "final"); the year is noted in the upper right corner of a variable (e.g. X^0 = exports in period 0)

---

[1] We use here the term "index" in its broad meaning. Technically, a measure would mostly be not a proper "index" but a "coefficient", a "ratio", and the like.

167

GDP = Gross Domestic Product

   X = Exports

   M = Imports

   D = Distance between pairs of countries

X_{ij}, M_{ij} = Exports and imports of good i by country j

$X_{.j}$, $M_{.j}$ = Aggregate exports and imports of good i by country j

$X_{.w}$, $M_{.w}$ = Aggregate world exports and imports

   | | = Absolute value (regardless of sign)

Indices

1. EC_j^1 = "Predicted" share of country j in world exports in period 1, based on commodity structure in period 0

$$= \sum_i \left[\left(\frac{X_{ij}}{X_{.j}} \right)^0 \left(\frac{X_{jw}}{X_w} \right)^1 \right]$$

2. RA_j^1 = Ratio of actual to "predicted" share in period 1

$$= \left(\frac{X_{.j}}{X_w} \right) \Big/ EC_j^1$$

3. EG_j^1 = "Predicted" share of country j in exports in period 1, based on geographic structure in period 0

$$= \sum_k \left[\left(\frac{M_k}{M_{.w}} \right)^1 \Big/ \left(\frac{M_w}{M_{.w}} \right)^0 \cdot \left(\frac{X_{kj}}{X_{.j}} \right)^0 \right]$$

4. $ET_j^{0,1}$ = "Predicted" change of foreign — trade ratio from period 0 to period 1

$$= \sum_i \left(\frac{R_i^1}{R_i^0} \cdot SH^0 \right), \text{ where}$$

R = share of sector i in GDP, and
SH^0 = share of exports in GDP.

5. D_{jk} = Index of dissimilarity of commodity export structures of two trade partners

$$= \frac{\sum_i \left| \dfrac{X_{ij}}{X_{.j}} - \dfrac{X_{ik}}{X_{.k}} \right|}{2}$$

6. IR_{jk} = Intensity ratio of trade between two trade partners

$$= \left(\frac{X_{ki}}{X_{.j}} \right) \cdot \left(\frac{M_{.k}}{M_w} \right)$$

7. GC_{jx} = Gini-Hirschman coefficient of commodity concentration of exports

$$= 100 \sqrt{\sum_i \frac{X_{ij}}{X_{.j}}}$$

8. IN_j = Index of intra-industry trade of country j

$$= 1 - \frac{\sum_i \left| \dfrac{X_{ij}}{M_{.j}} = \dfrac{M_{ij}}{M_{.j}} \right|}{2}$$

9. CN_{jk} = Index of compatibility of export-import structures of two trading partners

$$= 1 - \frac{\sum_i \left| \dfrac{X_{ij}}{X_{.j}} - \dfrac{M_{ik}}{M_{m.k}} \right|}{2}$$

10. DIS_j^x = Export-structure weighted mean distance of a country's exports

$$= \sum_k \left(\frac{X_{kj}}{X_{.j}} \cdot Dis._{kj} \right), \text{ where}$$

Dis_{kj} = Distance (in km) between j and k

11. DIS_j^k = Partner-imports weighted mean distance of a country's exports

$$= \sum_k \left(\frac{X_{kj}}{X_{.j}} \cdot Dis._{kj} \cdot \frac{M_k}{M_w} \right)$$

Annex B: Sources of Data (Listed by Tables)

Table 2.1, 2.2

World Bank databank

World Development Indicators. Series: Imports of goods and services (current US$)

World Development Indicators. Series: Imports GDP (current US$)

Extracted 2/4/2014

Table 2.3

World Bank databank

World Development Indicators. Series: Imports of goods and services (current US$)

World Development Indicators. Series: GDP (current US$)

Extracted 2/4/2014

Table 3.1, 3.2, 4.1, 4.2, 4.3, Annex table 4.1, Annex table 4.2, Table 5.1, Annex table 5.1, Table 8.1, Annex table 8.1, Table 9.1, 9.2, 9.3, 9.4, 9.5

UN COMTRADE Database

Imports and Exports by country, commodity and partner

Data by SITC

Extracted 29/3/2016 and 14/8/2017

Table 5.2

UN COMTRADE Database

Imports and Exports by country, commodity and partner

Data by SITC

Extracted 29/3/2016 and 14/8/2017

World Bank databank

World Bank national accounts data, and OECD National Accounts data files. Series: GDP Per Capita (current US$)

Extracted 28/7/2016

World Bank databank

World Bank national accounts data, and OECD National Accounts data files. Series: GDP (current US$)

Extracted 2/11/2016

Tables 6.1, 6.2, 6.3, 6.4, Annex table 6-B-1, Annex 6-1, Tables 7.1–7.2

UN COMTRADE Database

Imports and Exports by country, commodity and partner

Data by SITC

Extracted 28/2/2011

Distance — This is drawn from a file containing the great circle distance between capital cities (Gleditsch, Capdist.csv. — extracted from: http://ksgleditsch.com/data-5.html)

Table 8.2

UN Comtrade Database

Imports and Exports by country, commodity and partner

Data by SITC

Extracted 28/2/2011

World trade calculated as the sum of the exports of all countries represented in the UN Comtrade database who reported by SITC in 1962 or data by HS in 2010

Extracted on 23/11/2013

Bibliography

Anderson, J. E. (1979), "A Theoretical Function for the Gravity, Equation," *American Economic Review*, 69, 106–116.

Baldwin, Richard E. and Philippe Martin (1999), "Two Waves of Globalization: Superficial Similarities, Fundamental Differences," National Bureau of Economic Research Working Paper 6904.

Bergstrand, J. H. (1985), "Gravity Equation in International Trade: Some Microeconomic Foundations and Empirical Evidence," *Review of Economics and Statistics*, 67, 474–481.

Bergstrand, J. H. (1990), "The Heckscher-Ohlin-Samuelson Model, the Lynder Hypothesis, and the Determinants of Bilateral Intra-Industry Trade," *Economic Journal*, 100, 1216–1229.

Deutch, Karl W. and Alexander Eckstien (1961), "National Industrialization and the Declining Share of the International Economic Sector, 1880–1950," *World Politics*, 23, 267–299.

Disdier, Anne Célia and Keith Head (2008), "The Puzzling Persistence of the Distance Effect on Bilateral Trade," *Review of Economics and Statistics*, 90, 37–48.

Findlay, Ronald and Kevin H. O'Rourke (2007), *Power and Plenty*. Princeton: Princeton University Press.

Gini, Corrado (1927), *Variabilità et Mutabilità*, Bologna: Cuppini.

Grubel, H. G. and P. Lloyd (1975), *Intra-Industry Trade: The Theory and Measurement of International Trade in Differentiated Products*. New York: John Wiley & Sons.

Grynberg, R. (Ed.) (2006), *WTO at the Margins Small States and the Multilateral Trading System*. Cambridge: Cambridge University Press.

Helpman, E. and P. Krugman (1985), *Market Structure and Foreign Trade*. Cambridge, Mass: MIT Press.

Helpman, E., M. Melitz and Y. Rubinstein (2008), "Estimating Trade Flows, Trading Patterns and Trading Volumes," *Quarterly Journal of Economics*, 123, 441–448.

Hirschman, Albert O. (1945), *National Power and the Structure of Foreign Trade*. Berkly and Los Angeles: University of California Press. *Revised Edition* (1980): University of California Press.

Hirschman, Albert O. (1964), "The Paternity of an Index," *American Economic Review*, 54, 761–762.

Hummels D. (2001), "Towards a Geography of Trade Costs," Unpublished Manuscript, Purdue University.

Hummels, D., J. Ishii and Kei-Mu Yi (2001), "The Nature and Growth of Vertical Specialization in World Trade," *Journal of International Economics*, 54, 75–96.

Kleiman, E. (1976), "Trade and the Decline of Colonialism," *Economic Journal*, 86, 459–480.

Krugman, P. (1981), "Intra-Trade Specialization and the Gains from Trade," *Journal of Political Economy*, 89, 959–976.

Krugman, P. (2009), "The Increasing Returns Revolution in Trade and Geography," *American Economic Review*, 99, 561–571.

Kuznets, Simon (1959), *Six Lectures on Economic Growth*. New York: The Free Press.

Kuznets, Simon (1964), "Quantitative Aspects of the Economic Growth of Nations: Level and Structure of Foreign Trade," *Economic Development and Culture Change* (special supplement).

Lancaster, K. (1979), *Variety, Equity and Efficiency*. New York: Columbia University Press.

Linder, S. B. (1961), *An Essay on Trade and Transformation*. New York: John Wiley & Sons.

Linnemann, H. (1966). *An Econometric Study of International Trade Flows*, Amsterdam: Nort-Holand Publishing Co.

Michaely, M. (1962a), *Concentration in International Trade*. Amsterdam: North-Holand Publishing Co.

Michaely, M. (1962b), "Multilateral Balancing in International Trade," *American Economic Review*, 52, 685–702.

Michaely, M. (1968), "Patterns of Trade," in *International Encyclopedia of the Social Science*. The Macmillan Company and Free Press, 108–113.

Michaely, M. (1981), "Foreign Aid, Economic Structure and Dependence," *Journal of Development Economics*, 9, 313–330.

Michaely, M. (1984), *Trade, Income Levels and Dependence*, Amsterdam, New York and Oxford: North-Holland Publishing Co.

Michaely, M. (2009), *Trade Liberalization and Trade Performances (Revised Edition)*. Singapore: World Scientific Publishing Co.

Moneta, C. (1959), "The Estimation of Transportation Costs in International Trade," *Journal of Political Economy*, 67, 41–58.

Ohlin, B. (1933), *Intra-Regional and International Trade*. Cambridge, Mass.: Harvard University Press.

Redding, S. and A. J. Venables (2006), "The Economics of Isolation and Distance," Ch. 5 in *WTO at the Margins* (op. ct.), 145–163.

Rosecrance, R. and Arthur Stein (1973), "Interdependence: Myth or Reality?" *World Politics*, 26(1), 1–27.

Sombart, W. (1913), *Die Deutsche Volkswirtschaft im Neunzehnten Jahrhundert*. Berlin: G. Bondi.

Tinbergen, J. (1962), *Shaping the World Economy; Suggestions for an International Economic Policy*. New York: The Twentieth Century Fund.

Thorbecke, E. (1960), *The Tendency towards Regionalization in International Trade*, The Hague Martinus Nijhoff.

Names Index

Index

179

CPSIA information can be obtained
at www.ICGtesting.com
Printed in the USA
JSHW021724160120
3607JS00001B/3